FORMULA *for* HEALTH & SAFETY

GUIDANCE FOR SMALL AND MEDIUM-SIZED FIRMS IN THE CHEMICAL INDUSTRY

HSE BOOKS

© Crown copyright 1997
Application for reproduction should be made in writing to:
Copyright Unit, Her Majesty's Stationery Office,
St Clements House, 2-16 Colegate, Norwich NR3 1BQ

First published 1997

ISBN 0 7176 0996 0

HS(G)166

This guidance is issued by the Health and Safety Executive.
Following the guidance is not compulsory and you are free to take
other action. But if you do follow the guidance you will normally be
doing enough to comply with the law. Health and safety inspectors
seek to secure compliance with the law and may refer to this
guidance as illustrating good practice.

HSE gratefully acknowledges the help of Becker Industrial
Coatings Ltd, Speke, Liverpool, in the preparation of a number
of the photographs in this publication.

CONTENTS

FOREWORD

Small and medium-sized chemical businesses make up almost 80% of the 3600 chemical businesses in the UK. They have an important role in the industry.

Work with chemicals can be dangerous whether you are involved in manufacturing and processing or storage and distribution. Every year many people working in the industry suffer serious injuries or ill health which can sometimes be fatal. This results in pain and suffering for those affected, distress to their family and friends and sometimes public concern about the industry's ability to manage chemical risks.

Such incidents have costs in terms of absence, lost production, damage to buildings, plant or products, and often these costs are not covered by insurance.

Working safely is essential to your business - and the law demands it.

In this guidance book we aim to help you understand what you need to do and give sound practical advice for action. Working together helps everyone to work safely.

Dr Paul Davies
Head of the Chemical and Hazardous Installations Division (CHID) of HSE.

INTRODUCTION

This booklet is aimed at people who own, manage or work in small to medium-sized businesses that process, manufacture, store or distribute chemicals. However, the information in the booklet will also be of use to larger companies. It explains the principles of managing health and safety so that you can achieve safety in your workplace. It also identifies the main hazards in the industry and provides guidance on what you need to do to control risks at work.

It is divided into four sections:

Section 1: Managing health and safety. This section explains the principles of managing health and safety. It will help you get organised so that you can achieve high standards of health and safety in your workplace.

Section 2: Chemical industry hazards. This section identifies the main hazards in the chemical industry and ways of reducing the risks from these hazards.

Section 3: Chemical industry activities. This section covers some of the typical activities carried out in the chemical industry and gives guidance on the action you may need to take.

Section 4: Emergencies. This section shows what you should do in the event of an emergency.

Although this booklet covers much of the information you will need to run your business safely, it cannot cover everything. For more detailed information, you will find a list of relevant legislation and guidance at the end of each section.

It should be noted that this booklet doesn't cover the requirements of the Control of Industrial Major Accident Hazards Regulations 1984 (CIMAH). These Regulations apply to some chemical industry activities involving dangerous substances which can result in serious harm to people and the environment both within and beyond the immediate vicinity of the workplace.

The aim of the Regulations is to prevent major chemical industrial accidents and limit the consequences of those that do happen. They also require businesses to demonstrate that major accident hazards have been identified and are properly controlled. Depending on the nature and quantity of dangerous substances in use, a written safety report may be required.

-1-
MANAGING HEALTH AND SAFETY

Successful health and safety management in small and medium-sized chemical businesses means identifying serious and frequent risks and taking the right precautions to protect people from those risks.

It is not just about putting things right after they have gone wrong. It is more importantly about taking an organised approach to make sure mistakes don't happen in the first place.

3

MANAGING HEALTH AND SAFETY

The main steps you need to take are:

Set your policy

This will identify:

❏ who has health and safety responsibilities;

❏ how hazards are identified and risks assessed (this will be explained later);

❏ how these risks are controlled.

If you have five or more employees, your policy will need to be written down.

Organise your staff

This will include:

❏ checking that all employees have the skills to carry out their work safely. This will help identify any extra instruction or training needs;

❏ identifying people with particular health and safety duties and making sure they have the skills and resources to carry them out;

❏ making arrangements for any assistance you need to meet health and safety requirements (eg testing and examining pressure systems);

❏ discussing health and safety issues with your staff. They know what actually goes on in the workplace and can help develop practical solutions to problems;

❏ telling your staff about the risks involved with their work and the precautions they need to take.

Plan what you need to do

This will include:

- ❐ identifying hazards, assessing risks and deciding on controls;

- ❐ putting the controls in place;

- ❐ setting out what should be done in a situation of serious and imminent danger such as a spillage of a dangerous chemical (see Section 4);

- ❐ providing health surveillance where appropriate. For example, where your employees are exposed to lead or high noise levels (see pages 23-24).

Measure your performance

Some measures that can be used are:

before things go wrong:

- ❐ checking actual workplace standards against those you have set. For example, are chemicals properly stored, is local exhaust ventilation being used and is it working properly?

- ❐ have improvements identified in your risk assessment been put in place?

after things go wrong:

- ❐ you need to fully investigate accidents and any near misses to find out what happened.

Learn from experience

Measuring your performance provides information you can use to review what you do and decide where improvements can be made. Audits by your own staff or outsiders complement your measuring activities by looking to see if your policy, organisation and systems are actually achieving the right results.

ASSESSING RISKS

One of the key tasks in managing health and safety is to assess the risks in your workplace by carrying out a risk assessment.

What is a risk assessment?

It is an organised look at your work activities using the following five steps.

STEP 1: Look for the hazards.

STEP 2: Decide who may be harmed and how.

STEP 3: Evaluate the risks arising from the hazards and decide whether existing precautions are adequate or if more should be done.

STEP 4: Record your significant findings. (If you have fewer than five employees you don't have to record anything but you will probably find it easier if you do.)

STEP 5: Review your assessment from time to time and revise it if necessary.

KEY REFERENCE
Management of health and safety at work
Management of Health and Safety at work
Regulations 1992 Approved Code of
Practice L21 HSE Books 1992
ISBN 0 7176 0412 8

KEY REFERENCE
5 steps to risk assessment IND(G)163L
HSE Books 1994

MANAGING HEALTH AND SAFETY

Method of transfer	Possible source of spillage	
HFL transferred by enclosed pipeline system	Leaks from pipe joints and valves	INCREASING RISK
HFL transferred in enclosed containers	Spills during filling and emptying container	
HFL transferred in open containers	Spills during filling, emptying and transporting containers	

What do we mean by hazard and risk?

Hazard = Something that has potential to cause harm, eg machines, chemicals, electricity, etc.

Risk = The chance (big or small) of that harm actually being done.

For example, when a highly flammable liquid (HFL) is transferred from a storage tank to a mixing vessel, the hazard is the HFL and the main risk is that the HFL gets spilt and catches fire, causing injury. This risk will vary depending on how the HFL is transferred, see table above.

Using the five steps you need to choose the best approach for your situation. You may wish to carry out risk assessments for groups of hazards, eg:

☐ substances;

☐ machinery;

☐ electrical equipment;

☐ process equipment;

☐ access to workplaces.

Or it may be more appropriate to look at hazards associated with particular operations, eg:

☐ warehousing;

☐ production;

☐ packing;

☐ despatch;

☐ maintenance.

Or an entirely different approach may be suited to your situation.

Whatever approach you take, the risk assessment is one of the keys to improving health and safety standards in your workplace.

KEY REFERENCE
Five steps to successful health and safety:
Special help for directors and managers
IND(G)132L HSE Books 1992

Action plan

From your risk assessments you will have identified any areas that require improvements. You may find it useful to plan how the improvements can be made, by preparing a health and safety action plan. Following the chart below may help.

Prioritising

Prioritising your improvements is important as it is unlikely that you will be able to do everything at once.

Ensure high risk situations are dealt with quickly.

The diagram below may help you prioritise.

Identify the problems, ie using risk assessments

↓

Consider possible solutions to the problems ←

↓

Choose the best solutions

↓

Plan how to tackle the improvements

Prioritise the improvements

↓

Organise the people, time and money for the improvement

↓

Carry out the improvements

↓

Check how effective they have been and assess if further improvements are required

↓

Review progress

Feedback of information

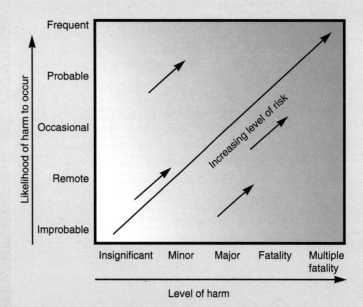

Level of harm

Once you have prioritised your improvements you can complete your action plan by saying what you will do and when.

The remaining sections of this booklet will help you to identify many of the hazards associated with the chemical industry and give guidance on how to reduce the risks.

The guidance will show many of the issues you should consider when carrying out your risk assessments and deciding on precautions.

RELEVANT LEGISLATION

The Health and Safety at Work etc Act 1974

The Management of Health and Safety at Work Regulations 1992

The Safety Representatives and Safety Committees Regulations 1977

The Health and Safety (Consultation with Employees) Regulations 1996

RELEVANT GUIDANCE

Management of health and safety at work Management of Health and Safety at Work Regulations Approved Code of Practice 1992 L21 HSE Books 1992 ISBN 0 7176 0412 8

Five steps to successful health and safety: Special help for directors and managers IND(G)132L HSE Books 1992

Successful health and safety management HS(G)65 HSE Books 1991 ISBN 0 7176 0425 X

5 steps to risk assessment IND(G)163L HSE Books 1994

Health risk management: A practical guide for managers in small and medium sized enterprises HS(G)137 HSE Books 1995 ISBN 0 7176 0905 7

-2-
CHEMICAL INDUSTRY HAZARDS

This section describes the main hazards in the chemical industry:

* *Fire*

* *Explosions*

* *Work-related ill health*

* *Equipment and the workplace*

* *Electricity*

9

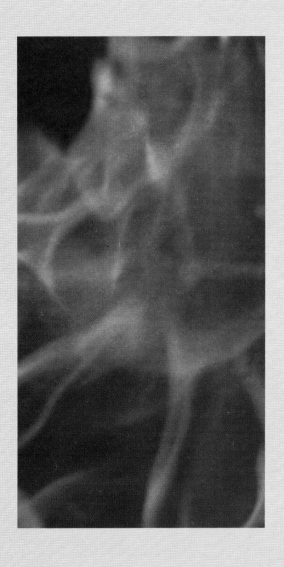

FIRE

Thirty-three people were sent to hospital and damages to company property were estimated at £4.25 m following a massive fire at a chemical factory in Yorkshire. The fire happened because incompatible substances were stored together. The accident could have been prevented.

A major fire broke out at an aerosol filling company after a build-up of leaking flammable propellant gas. Although the leak was identified, no training had been given in how to turn off the gas supply in an emergency. One person died, 14 were injured and the factory was virtually destroyed. This accident could also have been prevented.

These are just two of the many fires the chemical industry has suffered. Could your business survive the effects of a fire?

Often relatively simple precautions can either prevent a fire or reduce its consequences. Many fires result from a lack of awareness of the flammable properties of the materials in use, and consequently a lack of appropriate precautions.

The fire triangle

Three ingredients are needed for a fire: fuel, a supply of oxygen and an ignition source. These form the three corners of the fire triangle.

If any one of the corners is removed from the triangle, a fire will not break out. However it is not always possible to do this, so to reduce the chance of a fire occurring you need to control these three ingredients.

Considering the following will help you to control them.

FUEL
Flammable gases
Flammable liquids
Flammable solids
General combustible materials

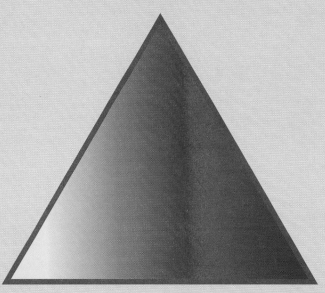

OXYGEN
Always present in the air
Additional sources from oxidising substances

IGNITION SOURCE
Hot surfaces
Electrical equipment
Static electricity
Smoking/naked flames

Fuel

☐ Identify the potential fuel sources, eg flammable gases, flammable liquids, flammable solids and general combustible materials such as packaging. Using information from labels, data sheets and your supplier will help.

☐ Where possible use materials which are non-flammable or of low flammability. In situations where this is not possible the severity of a fire can be reduced by keeping quantities of flammable materials in any one area to a minimum and storing them in safety containers such as fire-resisting bins or cupboards.

☐ Good housekeeping will help keep the amounts of combustible packaging and waste to a minimum.

Oxygen

☐ This is difficult to remove as it is always present in air. But remember oxygen enrichment of a fire will increase its ferocity, so keep oxidising substances away from fuel sources. The supplier's label and data sheet will help you to identify these.

Oxidising

Ignition sources

☐ There are many potential ignition sources in the workplace. Those present in areas where flammable materials are found need to be identified so they can be eliminated or controlled. Some typical ignition sources and possible controls are shown on page 12.

HAZARDS - FIRE

Ignition source	Control
Hot surfaces.	Insulation.
Electrical equipment.	Eliminate from areas of high risk. If this is not possible, use flameproof equipment. (See pages 30-32 on electricity).
Maintenance, eg welding, grinding, etc.	Where possible do it in an area away from flammable materials. If not possible, use a permit-to-work system. (See page 55).
Smoking.	No smoking policy/designated smoking area. Display no smoking signs.
Spontaneous ignition of certain materials.	Provide appropriate process and storage conditions.
Overheating bearings and slipping drive belts.	Proper maintenance and use of machines.
Static electricity.	Earthing. Use anti-static footwear and clothing.

Some examples of activities and associated fire hazards, risks and control measures are shown below.

Activity	Hazard	How risk may arise	Control measures
Handling bottles, cans, etc of flammable liquids, eg when packing products.	Flammable liquid.	Flammable liquid, leaks and catches fire.	• Use good quality packages designed to prevent leakage. • Train staff in safe handling of packages. • Elimination/control of ignition sources. • Spillage containment.
Filling containers with flammable liquids or solids.	Flammable liquid/solid.	Flammable liquid/solid is spilt and catches fire.	• Enclosed transfer system. • Elimination/control of ignition sources. • Local Exhaust Ventilation (LEV) to remove any flammable vapours. • Spillage containment.
Filling storage tanks with flammable liquids.	Flammable liquid.	Tank is overfilled, spilling flammable liquid which catches fire.	• Gauges and alarms, etc on tank. • Accurate instructions for tank filling. • Bunding of tanks to contain spillages. • Eliminate/control ignition sources.
Transfer of flammable liquid from storage tank to process area.	Flammable liquid.	Pipes or valves leak and and flammable liquid catches fire.	• Pipes and valves designed and constructed for the liquids being transferred. • Preventative maintenance carried out to prevent leaks. • Regular inspections for signs of damage/leaks.

KEY REFERENCE

The safe use and handling of flammable liquids
HS(G)140 HSE Books 1996 ISBN 0 7176 0967 7

12

How do you reduce the consequences of a fire?

The main aim is to take precautions to prevent a fire from starting. However, you also need to consider what can be done to minimise the consequences of a fire.

If a fire starts, two main matters need to be considered:

☐ how to slow the rate of the fire spreading, to allow time for evacuation of premises, and the emergency services to arrive;

☐ use emergency procedures to get people affected by the fire to safety.
(See Section 4 on Emergencies.)

How do you slow the spread of a fire?

For fire to keep burning and spreading it needs a supply of fuel and oxygen. If those are reduced, the fire does not spread so quickly.

You can reduce the fuel supply by limiting the combustible material available to burn, eg by:

☐ good housekeeping;

☐ keeping quantities of combustible material on site to a minimum;

☐ limiting the quantities of combustible material in high risk areas, eg production areas should only hold enough for a shift or half a day's production;

☐ controlling the amount of combustible material in one place by either storing it in separate areas, buildings, etc, or by separating stocks of combustible materials by appropriate separation distances;

☐ providing bunding or other suitable methods to contain any spillage of flammable liquids;

☐ providing ways of stopping flammable liquids and gases leaking by using remotely operated shut-off valves.

How do you reduce the oxygen supply?

☐ Don't store oxidising materials with combustible materials.

☐ Avoid oxygen enrichment of a fire by controlled storage and use of oxygen cylinders.

☐ As a fire increases it needs more oxygen. If a workplace is built to resist fire with fire-stopped doors, roof spaces, etc, the oxygen supply to the fire will be restricted, slowing down the burning rate of the fire.

☐ Use fire extinguishing mediums, eg water, foam CO_2, etc, to cut off the supply of oxygen to a fire. The correct mediums must be selected for the types of fire that are likely to occur.

Using fire detection and control systems such as fire and smoke detectors, alarms and sprinklers will also help slow the spread of a fire.

Your local fire authority will give you advice on the fire precautions you should take.

HAZARDS - FIRE

 **RELEVANT LEGISLATION**

The Health and Safety at Work etc Act 1974

The Fire Precautions Act 1971 (enforced by the Fire Authority)

The Fire Certificate (Special Premises) Regulations 1976

The Highly Flammable Liquids and Liquefied Petroleum Gases Regulations 1972

The Petroleum Consolidation Act 1928

RELEVANT GUIDANCE

Assessment of fire hazards from solid materials and the precautions required for their safe storage and use: A guide for manufacturers, suppliers, storekeepers and users HS(G)64 HSE Books 1991 ISBN 0 11 885654 5

Storage of packaged dangerous substances HS(G)71 HSE Books 1992 ISBN 0 11885989 7

The storage of flammable liquids in containers HS(G)51 HSE Books 1990 ISBN 0 7176 0481 0

The storage of flammable liquids in fixed tanks (up to 10 000 m³ total capacity) HS(G)50 HSE Books 1990 ISBN 0 11 885532 8

The storage of flammable liquids in fixed tanks (exceeding 10 000 m³ total capacity) HS(G)52 HSE Books 1991 ISBN 0 11 885538 7

The safe use and handling of flammable liquids HS(G)140 HSE Books 1996 ISBN 0 7176 0967 7

Safe working with flammable substances IND(G)227L HSE Books 1996 ISBN 0 7176 1154 X

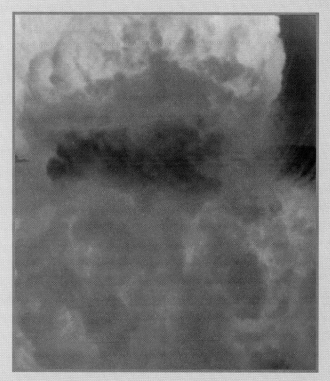

EXPLOSIONS

Explosions in the chemical manufacturing industry have a huge potential for causing injury to people and damage to plant, etc.

> *A man was killed and another injured in a violent explosion at a chemical factory in Greater Manchester. The accident happened when highly flammable hexane vapour was discharged into the factory from an overheating still as its cooling water supply failed. The vapour cloud exploded on ignition and caused extensive damage to the factory. If the flow of cooling water had been monitored and the still vented outside the building, the accident could have been prevented.*

Explosions generate a rapid release of energy which can cause injuries and damage from the blast, flame engulfment, exposure to harmful chemicals, thermal radiation, building collapse and flying debris.

There are several types of explosion. This part looks at the main types, what causes them, how to reduce the risk of an explosion and minimise the consequences of one.

KEY REFERENCE
A Guide to the Pressure Systems and Transportable Gas Containers Regulations 1989 HS(R)30 HSE Books 1990 ISBN 0 7176 0489 6

15

Pressure system explosions

These happen when pressure equipment such as reactors, pipework, distillation columns, autoclaves, steam boilers, gas storage tanks and air receivers, containing chemicals (eg liquids and gases) at high pressure fail and burst or explode. They may also occur in vessels that are not designed to take pressure but become pressurised accidentally.

Pressure equipment can fail if:

● it is not properly designed or constructed for the temperature and pressure it is to work at;

● the materials it is made from are not suitable;

● the process goes out of control;

● it does not have the appropriate safety devices;

● it is not properly maintained.

How you can reduce the risk

❑ Design and construct the equipment to suitable standards, (eg appropriate British Standards) taking account of the pressure and temperature at which it will operate.

❑ Ensure the materials the equipment is made from are suitable for the chemicals in the system.

❑ Fit suitable safety devices such as pressure relief valves, bursting discs, emergency shutdown systems, etc.

❑ Fit suitable instruments and control systems so the equipment and process can be properly controlled.

❑ Work to the correct operating procedures (eg with a batch process determine the correct quantities of chemicals and when they should be charged to the reactor).

❑ Provide operators with appropriate instruction and training on the safe operation of the equipment and process, including emergency procedures.

❑ Ensure that equipment is properly maintained and examined as required by the Pressure Systems and Transportable Gas Containers Regulations 1989.

HAZARDS - EXPLOSIONS

How you can reduce the consequences

☐   If practicable, site the pressure system where it is not likely to affect people, eg away from thoroughfares and working areas.

☐   Vent pressure relief valves and bursting discs to a safe area.

☐   Prepare emergency procedures to safeguard people at risk in an emergency (see Section 4).

Gas/vapour explosions

These explosions happen when a flammable gas or vapour mixes with air to form a flammable cloud that comes in contact with a suitable ignition source. An explosion may be initiated in plant or equipment, within the confines of a building or even in the open if there is enough material or turbulence within the cloud.

The severity of the explosion largely depends on:

- the ratio of flammable gas/vapour to air in the cloud. There are lower limits (LEL = lower explosive limit) below which insufficient gas/vapour is available for the cloud to ignite and upper limits (UEL = upper explosive limit), where there is insufficient oxygen for the cloud to ignite due to high amounts of gas/vapour in the cloud;

- whether or not the gas/vapour cloud is confined in any way. A cloud formed on open ground is less likely to produce a damaging explosion, (it will however produce damaging heat radiation and fire engulfment effects) than a cloud confined in a building, process vessel, etc. In these cases there is little chance for the explosion to vent, resulting in blast damage to buildings, plant, etc with projectiles being produced, injuring people and releasing more flammable materials;

- the amount of turbulence created in the cloud. The more turbulence, the more severe the explosion;

- the amount of fuel available to form a flammable cloud; and

- for explosions within plant, the bursting pressure of that plant.

A gas/vapour cloud can be produced by:

- leaks from damaged/poorly maintained storage tanks/vessels/containers;

- leaks from damaged/poorly maintained process equipment;

- releases from storage vessels and process equipment by poor operating procedures, and untrained operators;

- unplanned variation in process reaction causing a cloud to form in the process vessel;

- leaks/releases from inappropriately designed equipment and equipment used for a purpose it wasn't designed for;

- leaks/releases when carrying out maintenance work.

How you can reduce the risk

☐   Identify all substances on site that could result in a flammable gas/vapour cloud. Consider raw materials, intermediate products of reactions, finished products and waste products.

☐   Where possible, eliminate substances that can result in flammable gas/vapour clouds or substitute them with less flammable alternatives, and keep quantities on site to a minimum.

☐   Where flammable liquids are being processed, operating temperatures should be reduced if possible to minimise the risk of forming a flammable vapour cloud.

KEY REFERENCE
The safe use and handling of flammable liquids HS(G)140 HSE Books 1996
ISBN 0 7176 0967 7

KEY REFERENCE
Lift-trucks in potentially flammable atmospheres HS(G)113 HSE Books 1996
ISBN 0 7176 0706 2

❒ Ensure equipment used to store and process these substances has been designed for its intended purpose and is maintained appropriately to prevent leaks.

❒ Design and operate processes so that gas/vapour mixtures within the plant are kept outside their flammable ranges.

❒ Fit suitable instruments and control systems so the equipment and process can be properly controlled.

❒ Provide accurate safe operating procedures for storage and processing, etc.

❒ Train and instruct operators in safe operating procedures.

❒ Remove/control ignition sources in areas where it is foreseeable a flammable gas/vapour cloud may form.

❒ Use exhaust ventilation to remove gas/vapour as it is produced, preventing a cloud from forming.

❒ Fit alarms and protection systems to detect when atmospheres in vulnerable areas approach the LEL. (These are typically set at 25% of the LEL) and put the plant into a safe state.

❒ Control all maintenance work on any plant that has contained flammable substances (see pages 52-56).

How you can reduce the consequences

❒ Locate processes and storage facilities that may result in the formation of a flammable gas/vapour cloud in well ventilated areas and away from the main workforce.

❒ Fit explosion relief vents in equipment/areas where explosions may occur to allow the explosion to vent to a safe area.

❒ Reduce the amount of projectiles available in the event of an explosion by good housekeeping, building layout, etc.

❒ Consider the location and explosion proofing control rooms where appropriate.

❒ Prepare emergency procedures to safeguard people at risk in an emergency (see Section 4).

Dust explosions

These happen when the dust of a combustible solid is dispersed in air forming a flammable dust cloud, which will ignite and explode on contact with an ignition source. The severity of the explosion will depend on the ratio of dust to air in the cloud, the type of dust the cloud is made of and the confinement of the cloud. As with gas/vapour clouds, there are lower limits below which insufficient dust is available for the cloud to ignite, ie the LEL.

An important characteristic of dust explosions is that a small initial explosion can disturb accumulations of dust in the factory, particularly from upper surfaces. This adds more combustible dust to the cloud which results in a much larger and more violent secondary explosion.

Several processes in the industry are designed to produce dusts (eg grinding and milling). Consequently the plant will create explosible clouds inside itself. As a result incidents can start within the process plant, often beginning as a fire.

A dust cloud can be produced by:

● any movement of dusts within a process;

● dust leaking from process equipment;

● dust produced at loading hoppers, etc;

● dust dislodged from accumulations, particularly on upper surfaces within the building;

● dust leaking from sacks and bags.

KEY REFERENCE
The safe handling of combustible dusts: Precautions against explosions HS(G)103 HSE Books 1994 ISBN 0 7176 0725 9

HAZARDS - EXPLOSIONS

How you can reduce the risk

❒ Identify all substances used that could lead to a flammable dust cloud and ensure you understand their properties, in particular their thermal stability. Consider raw materials, intermediate products of processes, finished products and waste products.

❒ Where possible, eliminate substances that can result in flammable dust clouds being formed.

❒ Use a less combustible substance or the substance in a different form, eg granules, liquids, pastes, instead of powder.

❒ Add dedusting agents to the substance.

❒ Prevent foreign material from entering the equipment.

❒ Prevent overheating caused by flow blockages and badly maintained equipment.

❒ Ensure equipment being used has been designed and maintained to minimise the production of unwanted dust.

❒ Ensure operating procedures have been produced to keep unwanted dust production to a minimum.

❒ Train operators in safe operating procedures.

❒ Remove/control ignition sources in areas where it is foreseeable a flammable dust cloud may form.

❒ Use exhaust ventilation to remove any unwanted dust to a safe place.

How you can reduce the consequences

❒ Clean the premises regularly to prevent a build-up of dust that may fuel a secondary explosion, paying particular attention to upper surfaces.

❒ Locate processes that lead to flammable dust clouds away from the main workforce.

❒ Locate plant in open-sided buildings.

❒ Fit explosion relief vents in equipment/areas to allow an explosion to vent to a safe place.

❒ Reduce the amount of projectiles available in the event of an explosion by good housekeeping and building layout.

❒ Prepare emergency procedures to safeguard people at risk in an emergency (see Section 4). In particular these should deal with suspected fire in the plant to prevent it escalating into an explosion.

Energetic substances

When considering explosion hazards it is important to remember that some substances used and produced in the industry have energetic or energy releasing properties. Typically these substances may be:

● unstable at or below normal room temperature;

● stable at normal room temperature but react with air or moisture;

● stable at room temperature but decompose on heating (possibly after a long time).

Decomposition of these substances can happen, eg due to heat, friction or impact. When they decompose they can result in a fire or explosion with subsequent missiles and blast effects similar to those described under the gas/vapour explosions heading.

The amounts of these substances on site should be kept to a minimum with consideration given to the use of less hazardous substances. Where these substances are used the process and equipment should not lead to the conditions that will cause a decomposition.

KEY REFERENCE
Energetic and spontaneously combustible substances: Identification and safe handling
HS(G)131 HSE Books 1995
ISBN 0 7176 0893 X

18

RELEVANT LEGISLATION

The Health and Safety at Work etc Act 1974

The Management of Health and Safety at Work Regulations 1992

The Provision and Use of Work Equipment Regulations 1992

The Workplace (Health, Safety and Welfare) Regulations 1992

The Pressure Systems and Transportable Gas Containers Regulations 1989

The Factories Act 1961 section 31

The Equipment and Protective Systems for Use in Potentially Explosive Atmospheres Regulations 1996

RELEVANT GUIDANCE

The safe handling of combustible dusts: Precautions against explosions HS(G)103 HSE Books 1994 ISBN 7176 0725 9

Energetic and spontaneously combustible substances: Identification and safe handling HS(G)131 HSE Books 1995 ISBN 0 7176 0893 X

A Guide to the Pressure Systems and Transportable Gas Containers Regulations 1989 HS(R)30 HSE Books 1990 ISBN 0 7176 0489 6

Written schemes of examination Pressure Systems and Transportable Gas Containers Regulations 1989 IND(G)178L HSE Books 1994

The safe use and handling of flammable liquids HS(G)140 HSE Books 1996 ISBN 0 7176 0967 7

Out of control: Why control systems go wrong and how to prevent failure HSE Books 1995 ISBN 0 7176 0847 6

Programmable electronic systems: An introductory guide HSE Books 1987 ISBN 0 7176 1278 3

Programmable electronic systems: General technical guidelines HSE Books 1987 ISBN 0 7176 0545 0

Lift-trucks in potentially flammable atmospheres HS(G)113 HSE Books 1996 ISBN 0 7176 0706 2

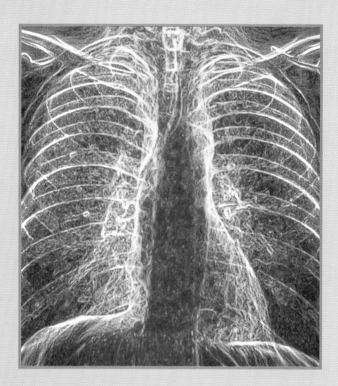

WORK-RELATED ILL HEALTH

Health problems caused by work will often develop unnoticed, unlike the effects of an accident which will usually be noticed quickly. Awareness of these problems together with the correct precautions can reduce the risk of work-related ill health.

There are three main problem areas within the chemical industry:

- exposure to hazardous substances;

- noise; and

- manual handling activities.

These problems may cause illnesses such as occupational asthma, dermatitis, cancer, hearing loss, back injuries and upper limb disorders.

KEY REFERENCE

Health risk management: A practical guide for managers in small and medium sized enterprises HS(G)137 HSE Books 1995 ISBN 0 7176 0905 7

Using hazardous substances

The industry uses a wide variety of hazardous substances on a daily basis, substances which are capable of causing a wide range of health problems. Some may happen quickly while others can build up over time, eg:

- short term exposure to chlorine causes irritation to the throat and lungs at very low concentrations. Exposure at higher concentrations can be fatal after a few breaths;

- exposure over a long period of time to chromate compounds can lead to skin ulceration and may cause cancer.

What substances are hazardous to health?

- Those labelled as very toxic, toxic, corrosive, harmful or irritant. Also, micro-organisms, dusts, fumes and other materials can harm people's health.

Hazardous substances may be found as:

- raw materials;

- intermediate products of processes/reactions;

- finished products;

- by products;

- waste products.

Hazardous substances may come in the form of:

- solids (includes powders, granules, dust, etc);
- liquids;
- gases and vapours.

People may be affected by:

- inhalation of dusts, gases or vapours, eg exposure to cadmium dusts/fumes can cause lung disease and even kidney damage;

- ingestion of solids, dusts, liquids, eg ingestion of inorganic mercury salts can cause mercury poisoning;

- skin contact with solids, dusts, liquids. Some substances may pass through the skin, causing ill health while others may injure the skin, eg skin contact with organic solvents can cause dermatitis.

Who may be affected?

- Production staff;
- Packing staff;
- Warehouse staff;
- Maintenance staff;
- Contractors;
- Cleaners.

The effect on people will usually depend on how hazardous the substance is, the level of exposure and the length of time they are exposed to it.

For many substances with dusts, vapours or gases that may be inhaled, exposure limits have been set which should not normally be exceeded. They are listed in booklet EH40 *Occupational Exposure Limits* which is updated annually.

With such a variety of hazardous substances being used at all stages of the production cycle, you need to ensure the risks from them are properly controlled.

How you can reduce the risk

- ☐ Identify the hazardous substances used on site, not forgetting those used in non-production work such as maintenance. Identification is helped by using suppliers' information (eg labels and safety data sheets), your knowledge, previous experience, and guidance from HSE, trade associations and industry.

- ☐ Assess what risks there are for the way each substance is used. Consider how exposure may happen, who may be affected and what controls are already in place. The most hazardous substance you have may not produce the greatest risks. For example, a toxic chemical handled in a totally enclosed

system from storage to processing and packing results in a low risk. However, a mild irritant handled with inadequate precautions may lead to dermatitis, affecting a large number of people, and is potentially a higher risk.

- ☐ If a hazardous substance has an occupational exposure limit (see EH40), ensure that limit is not exceeded.

- ☐ Consider what else can be done to reduce the risk further.

Using the following sequence may help identify how you can reduce risks even more.

Can any hazardous substances be eliminated altogether, eg by changes in the processes or the product specification?

↓

Can any hazardous substances be replaced by a less hazardous alternative or in a less hazardous form, eg can dusty powders be replaced by granules or liquids?

↓

Can exposure to the hazardous substances be reduced by engineering controls such as Local Exhaust Ventilation (LEV), enclosure of all or part of a process, automation of the process or reducing the time people are exposed?

↓

Is personal protective equipment (PPE) needed? If PPE is to be used, check that it is of a standard high enough to give protection against the hazards of the substance in use. Make sure the user knows how to use it and that it fits them properly. You must also make sure the equipment is cleaned and maintained so it is still efficient and fit to use.
(**Note:** You should only use PPE if it is not reasonably practicable to control exposure in the ways already outlined.)

↓

Decide what improvements can be made, introduce them and check that they have worked.

KEY REFERENCE
General COSHH ACoP Control of Substances Hazardous to Health Regulations 1994 L5 HSE Books 1995 ISBN 0 7176 0819 0

21

KEY REFERENCE
Step by step guide to COSHH assessment HS(G)97 HSE Books 1993 ISBN 0 11 886379 7

Some examples of hazardous substances, risks and controls are shown below.

Activity	Hazard	How risk may arise	Control measures
Drumming off corrosive liquids, eg from a bulk supply or production vessel.	Corrosive liquid.	Chemical burns to the operator splashed by the liquid.	• Use an enclosed transfer system to fill drums. • Use PPE selected to protect the user from the corrosive liquid.
Charging a mixing vessel with a harmful powder.	Harmful dust from powder.	Inhalation of the dust which affects the respiratory system.	• Use a less harmful powder. • Use the same material in a different form, eg granules, pellets or liquid. • Use LEV. • Use PPE selected to protect the user from the dust.
Maintenance work on an acid pump.	Acid remaining in the pump.	Chemical burns to maintenance staff.	• Isolate the pump from the acid supply. • Clean and purge the pump. • Control the work by a permit-to-work (PTW) system.

Noise

Regular exposure to high noise levels can cause irreversible deafness. The longer you are exposed and the higher the noise level, the greater the damage to your hearing. There are several noisy processes carried out in the chemical industry that have the potential to damage your hearing, eg milling, grinding, bottling, etc.

How you can reduce the risk

If you or your workforce are exposed to high noise levels you need to take steps to control exposure to a safe level. This can be done by the following:

❒ Identify areas where noise may be a problem. (As a guide, if you have to shout to someone two metres away to be understood, noise levels are probably high enough to damage hearing.)

❒ Have a noise assessment of these areas carried out by a competent person to identify the source of the noise, level of exposure and the people affected.

❒ Take action to reduce exposure to noise where it has been identified as a problem. This is best achieved by controlling it at source. Wearing ear protection should be a last resort.

KEY REFERENCE
Noise at work: Guidance on the Noise at Work Regulations 1989 Noise guides 1 and 2 HSE Books 1989 ISBN 0 7176 0454 3

Noise at work: Noise assessment information and control Noise guides 3-8 HSE Books 1990 ISBN 0 11 885430 5

Following the sequence below will help you to reduce exposure.

> Eliminate the source of the noise, where you can.
>
> ↓
>
> Choose quiet machines or processes when selecting production methods.
>
> ↓
>
> Enclose noisy machines and processes with sound insulating enclosures or put them in separate rooms.
>
> ↓
>
> Arrange work so that workers aren't in the noisy area.
>
> ↓
>
> Reduce the duration of exposure by job rotation or by providing a noise refuge such as an acoustically treated control room.
>
> ↓
>
> Ensure operators in noisy areas wear appropriate hearing protection and are given information and training on how to use it.
>
> ↓
>
> Check that the improvements made have reduced noise exposure and assess if more changes are needed.

Manual handling

Lifting, carrying and moving loads by hand are among the main causes of injury at work. Handling activities like these can cause injuries to the neck, shoulders, back or arms. Where the load is heavy or the handling conditions are poor, one bad manoeuvre can be enough to cause the injury. Cumulative damage can also build up over a long period, particularly when working repetitively with lighter loads.

Many operations in the chemical industry involve handling heavy loads. Tasks such as charging of reactors and mixing vessels with raw materials pose particular problems for the back. Repetitive tasks involving lighter loads such as the packaging of finished products can typically affect the shoulders, arms and hands (commonly known as Upper Limb Disorders).

How you can reduce the risk

The first step is to identify the tasks where injuries may occur, then decide what action is appropriate. This may involve changing what the workers do, how they do it or improving their manual handling skills. Solutions often include elements of all three and can involve:

☐ reorganising the task to eliminate or reduce manual handling;

☐ automating or mechanising the task to eliminate or reduce manual handling;

☐ using lifting aids to minimise the amount of manual handling;

☐ ordering materials that have to be manually handled in packages of easily handled sizes;

☐ planning work breaks or introducing job rotation to avoid long periods of repetitive work;

☐ training your employees in good handling techniques.

After you have made improvements check that they have reduced the chance of injury from manual handling tasks and assess if more changes are needed.

Checking for ill health

Carrying out health checks on your employees is a useful way to identify if the work they are doing is affecting their health.

In some cases, eg work with lead, vinyl chloride monomer, etc, specific health checks are required by law. With some hazards specialist help may be needed. For example, if you work with known respiratory sensitisers or high noise levels, you may need periodic checks on lung function or hearing which will require specialist help. In many cases checks can be fairly simple and will not need a doctor or nurse to carry them out.

KEY REFERENCE

Health surveillance under COSHH: Guidance for employers HSE Books 1990
ISBN 0 7176 0491 8

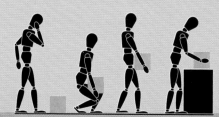

KEY REFERENCE

Manual handling: Manual Handling Operations Regulations 1992 Guidance on regulations
L23 HSE Books 1992 ISBN 0 7176 0411 X

HAZARDS - WORK-RELATED ILL HEALTH

What you can do

☐ Check whether there are any known health risks from the work you do and let your employees know about them and the precautions they should take.

☐ Listen to complaints about ill health. Consider what is happening if there are a number of similar complaints or there is a lot of sickness absence in the same area or as a result of the same activity.

☐ Encourage your employees to inform you of ill health problems that may have arisen from their work.

☐ Encourage your employees to tell their doctor about the work they do if they think it may be affecting their health, and to take with them any relevant information such as safety data sheets for the substances they work with.

 RELEVANT LEGISLATION

The Health and Safety at Work etc Act 1974

The Management of Health and Safety at Work Regulations 1992

The Control of Substances Hazardous to Health Regulations 1994

The Noise at Work Regulations 1989

The Manual Handling Operations Regulations 1992

The Personal Protective Equipment at Work Regulations 1992

The Control of Asbestos at work Regulations 1987

The Control of Lead at Work Regulations 1980

RELEVANT GUIDANCE

General COSHH ACoP The Control of Substances Hazardous to Health Regulations 1994 HSE Books 1995 ISBN 0 7176 0819 0

Health risk management: A practical guide for managers in small and medium sized enterprises HS(G)137 HSE Books 1995 ISBN 0 7176 0905 7

Occupational exposure limits EH40/97 HSE Books 1997 ISBN 0 7176 1315 1

Step by step guide to COSHH assessment HS(G)97 HSE Books 1993 ISBN 0 11 886379 7

COSHH: A brief guide to employers IND(G)136L HSE Books 1996 ISBN 0 7176 1189 2

COSHH: A guide to assessment IAC L62 HSE Books 1992

Health surveillance under COSHH: Guidance for employers HSE Books 1990 ISBN 0 7176 0491 8

Preventing asthma at work: How to control respiratory sensitisers L55 HSE Books 1994 ISBN 0 7176 0661 9

Noise at work: Guidance on the Noise at Work Regulations 1989 Noise guides 1 and 2 HSE Books 1989 ISBN 0 7176 0454 3

Noise at work: Noise assessment information and control Noise guides 3-8 HSE Books 1990 ISBN 0 11 885430 5

One hundred practical applications of noise reduction methods HSE Books 1983 ISBN 0 11 883691 9

Introducing the noise at work regulations: A brief guide to the new requirements controlling noise at workplaces IND(G)75L HSE Books 1989

Ear protection in noisy firms IND(G)200L HSE Books 1995

Sound solutions HS(G)138 HSE Books 1995 ISBN 0 7176 0791 7

Manual handling: Manual Handling Operations Regulations 1992 Guidance on regulations L23 HSE Books 1992 ISBN 0 7176 0411X

Manual handling: Solutions you can handle HS(G)115 HSE Books 1994 ISBN 0 7176 0693 7

A pain in your workplace: Ergonomic problems and solutions HS(G)121 HSE Books 1994 ISBN 0 7176 0668 6

Getting to grips with manual handling: A short guide for employers IND(G)143L HSE Books 1993

Personal protective equipment at work: Guidance on regulations L25 HSE Books 1992 ISBN 0 7176 0415 2

A short guide to PPE IND(G)174L HSE Books 1994

What your doctor needs to know IND(G)116L HSE Books 1992

24

EQUIPMENT AND THE WORKPLACE

The chemical industry experiences the same types of accidents from equipment and workplace hazards as the general manufacturing industry. Although these may be less dramatic than fires and explosions which catch the public eye, their prevention still has to be managed.

Two examples of such accidents are shown below.

A man suffered serious injuries to his left hand as he reached into the unguarded inlet of a milling machine to clear a blockage of chemicals. A simple guard that could have prevented the accident was fitted immediately afterwards. It should have been there all the time.

A chemical process operator died from serious injuries received after falling five metres (5 m) onto a concrete floor through a gap in a first floor work platform. The floor panels hadn't been secured to the supporting beams and became displaced, leaving the gap in the floor. It would have taken very little time to secure the panels in place.

HAZARDS - EQUIPMENT AND THE WORKPLACE

Work equipment

A wide range of equipment is used in the chemical manufacturing industry, eg mixers, reactors, grinders, hoists, fork-lift trucks, etc. All of them are capable of causing injury to those using them or working near them if the proper precautions aren't taken.

What can cause injuries?

- Being entangled on rotating parts of equipment;

- Being trapped between moving parts of equipment;

- Being trapped between moving equipment or parts of equipment and buildings or other fixed objects;

- Being struck by material ejected from equipment;

- Being struck by moving equipment or parts of it;

- Being burnt from hot parts of equipment being used.

So you need to assess the equipment in use in your factory (not forgetting equipment that may only be used occasionally) for these hazards and then consider the following.

Who may be affected?

- Operators of the equipment;

- Those working near the equipment;

- Maintenance and repair workers;

- Contractors and other visitors to the site.

When can the risks arise?

- Setting up the equipment;

- Operating the equipment;

- Cleaning the equipment;

- Carrying out maintenance and repairs on the equipment.

How you can reduce the risk

- ☐ Ensure the equipment selected is suitable for the work to be done and the conditions in which it is to work.

- ☐ Prevent access to dangerous parts of the equipment. When doing this consider the following:

  - fixed guards enclosing the dangerous parts must be used if practicable, and fixed in place, eg with screws or nuts and bolts;

  - think about the best materials to use. Plastic may be easy to see through but can be easily damaged. Where wire mesh or similar materials are used, make sure the holes are not large enough to allow access to the dangerous parts;

  - if you have to go near to dangerous parts regularly and fixed guards are not practicable, you must use other methods, eg interlock the guard so that the machine cannot start before the guard is closed and cannot be opened when the machine is moving;

  - in some cases trip systems such as photo electric devices, pressure sensitive mats or automatic guards may be used instead of fixed or interlocked guards if these are not practicable.

- ☐ Maintain guards in good working order.

- ☐ Ensure operators of the equipment are trained in its safe use, paying particular attention to inexperienced staff such as temporary or young workers.

- ☐ Ensure you have safe procedures for cleaning, maintaining and repairing the equipment using isolation and permit-to-work (PTW) procedures where appropriate. (See pages 52-57 on maintenance and modifications to the plant and processes.)

Now decide on any improvements you need to make, carry them out and check that they have worked.

KEY REFERENCE
Work equipment: Guidance on regulations
L22 HSE Books 1992 ISBN 0 7176 0414 4

HAZARDS - EQUIPMENT AND THE WORKPLACE

Workplace access

Accidents from gaining access around the workplace can be divided into four categories: slips, trips, falls and those from workplace transport. You need to assess your workplace for places where these accidents may happen. Considering the following points may help.

Slips: Many substances used in chemical manufacturing and processing can be very slippery. If they are allowed to contaminate access routes such as walkways or steps, this can result in a slipping hazard. Slips may also be caused by walkways or steps, etc with surfaces that have little grip.

Trips: These are often caused by poor housekeeping, for example, walkways being obstructed by raw materials, finished products, or waste materials, etc. Badly routed cables and pipes together with poorly maintained access routes provide more tripping hazards.

Falls: Access is needed at height for many purposes, eg routinely charging reactors or mixing vessels, maintaining and cleaning equipment and buildings. Even falls from modest heights can cause serious injuries, especially if the fall is onto equipment or a chemical.

Workplace transport: Vehicles such as fork-lift trucks, lorries and vans transporting goods to and from the site are in frequent use at most chemical manufacturing and processing sites. Accidents from them usually involve people being struck or run over by moving vehicles, falling from vehicles, being struck by objects falling from vehicles, or the vehicles overturning.

How you can reduce the risk

First identify where in your workplace slips, trips, falls and transport accidents could occur and then decide how the chance of them happening can be reduced. Considering the following points may help.

Slips

❐ Design/modify equipment to reduce spillages and leaks.

❐ Set out work procedures that will reduce spillages.

❐ Have good housekeeping procedures for cleaning up spillages.

❐ Use anti-slip surfaces and footwear.

Trips

❐ Route cables and pipes away from access routes.

❐ Site equipment with adequate room around it for the intended access.

❐ Construct and maintain access routes properly, eg are steps and handrails in the correct places? Are any holes in walkways repaired straight away?

❐ Keep access routes free of obstructions such as raw materials, finished products and waste materials. Consider marking main walkways to ensure they are kept clear.

Falls

❐ How often is access needed? Can you avoid the need for work at height? If you need frequent access make sure there is permanent access via steps or ladders to a permanent work platform. If you rarely need access, portable ladders, scaffolds or mobile elevating work platforms can be used instead. For the more physical work activities, platforms are preferable to ladders.

KEY REFERENCE
Workplace health, safety and welfare
Workplace Regulations Approved Code
of Practice L24 HSE Books 1992
ISBN 0 7176 0413 6

27

❑ Secure guard rails should be fitted to any open edges where a person may fall and suffer a serious injury. For example, all edges 2 m or more high and any lower than 2 m, where the risk of injury is increased (eg by traffic routes, sharp surfaces or dangerous machines, etc) should be guarded.

❑ Maintain all ladders, steps, handrails and work platforms in a safe condition.

Workplace transport

❑ Check the layout of your vehicle routes. Are vehicles and pedestrians kept safely apart and are there suitable pedestrian crossing points? Are the routes suitable for the types of vehicles using them? They need to be wide enough and well maintained.

❑ Is there a safe means of access on and off the vehicles, eg to the driving position, to road tanker tops, etc?

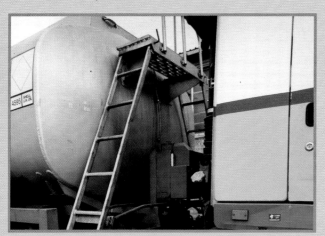

❑ Check that your vehicles are well maintained and drivers carry out basic safety checks before using them.

❑ Do your training procedures ensure that drivers are capable of carrying out their work in a safe and responsible manner?

Now decide on any improvements you need to make, carry them out and check they have worked.

Don't forget access around your factory is not only used by you and your workforce, but also by visitors to the site, such as contractors and customers. You have responsibilities for their safety while they are on site.

RELEVANT LEGISLATION

The Health and Safety at Work etc Act 1974

The Provision and Use of Work Equipment Regulations 1992

The Workplace (Health, Safety and Welfare) Regulations 1992

RELEVANT GUIDANCE

Work equipment: Guidance on regulations L22
HSE Books 1992 ISBN 0 7176 0414 4

Workplace health, safety and welfare Workplace Regulations Approved Code of Practice L24
HSE Books 1992 ISBN 0 7176 0413 6

Workplace transport safety HS(G)136
HSE Books 1995 ISBN 0 7176 0935 9

Managing vehicle safety at the workplace
IND(G)190L HSE Books 1995 ISBN 0 7176 0982 0

Rider operated lift trucks: Operator training ACoP 26
HSE Books 1988 ISBN 0 7176 0474 8

Safety in working with lift trucks HS(G)6
HSE Books 1993 ISBN 0 11 886395 9

Slips, trips and falls HSE Books 1996
ISBN 0 7176 1156 6

KEY REFERENCE
Workplace transport safety HS(G)136
HSE Books 1995 ISBN 0 7176 0935 9

> A highly flammable liquid was being added to a centrifuge via plastic pipework when an explosion occurred, followed by a serious fire. It was concluded that static electricity generated by the flow of the liquid through the pipes raised a spark that ignited the flammable vapours from the liquid.
>
> The plastic pipes were replaced with earthed metal pipes and earthing is now checked regularly.

ELECTRICITY

Electricity is vital to the efficient operation of the chemical industry, but if the supply and equipment is not installed and maintained properly, it can create severe hazards in the workplace.

Hazards

The three main hazards associated with electricity are:

- contact with live parts causing shock and burns (normal mains voltage can kill);

- fires started from faulty installations; and

- fire or explosions caused by electrical equipment or static electricity igniting flammable gases, vapours, mists or dusts.

KEY REFERENCE
Memorandum of Guidance on the Electricity at Work Regulations 1989 HS(R)25
HSE Books 1989 ISBN 0 11 883963 2

How you can reduce the risk

The main requirement with electricity is to ensure that all electrical systems, eg wiring installations, fixed equipment, portable equipment, generators, battery sets, etc, are of proper construction and maintained, so far as is reasonably practicable, to prevent danger.

The following precautions will help you achieve this.

- ❏ Check that equipment in use (and any proposed new equipment) is of a suitable design and construction for the work it is intended to do and the environment in which it is to be used. For example, plugs, sockets and switches for use in a factory should be of an industrial, not domestic, type. Equipment for use in a potentially flammable atmosphere will need to be to a suitable explosion protected standard.

- ❏ Develop a programme for maintenance of your electrical systems. Regular inspection and, where appropriate, testing are important parts of such a programme. The frequency and nature of the inspection and testing will depend on several factors, including the type of equipment (in general portable equipment will need more frequent inspections and tests than fixed equipment), the environment in which it is used and the work it is doing.

- ❏ The information gained from the inspection and testing of your equipment will help decide on maintenance work required. It will help if you keep records of the inspections, tests and maintenance work done.

☐ Check that any electricians or electrical contractors you use are competent for the work they are to do. Levels of qualification established by the Electrical Joint Industries Board may be of help, but check that the qualifications are relevant. A fully qualified TV technician is unlikely to be competent to install equipment in a chemical factory.

If you own portable (and transportable) electric equipment, you are recommended to encourage the equipment users to carry out a visual check for signs of damage before they use it. This is in addition to the routine formal inspection and testing of the equipment.

Typical signs to look for are:

● exposed bare wires;

● damage (apart from light scuffing) to the cable sheath;

● damage to the plug, eg the casing could be cracked or the pins bent;

● inadequate joints in the cable, eg taped joints;

● the outer sheath of the cable not being secured in the plug or equipment. The coloured insulation of the internal wires should not be showing;

● whether the equipment has been used in conditions it wasn't suitable for, eg is it wet or contaminated with dirt or chemicals;

● damage to the casing of the equipment, eg some parts could be loose or screws could be missing;

● evidence of overheating, eg burn marks or discoloration.

KEY REFERENCE
Maintaining portable and transportable electrical equipment HS(G)107 HSE Books 1994
ISBN 0 7176 0715 1

FLAMMABLE OR EXPLOSIVE ATMOSPHERES

There are two main sources of electricity that can provide a source of ignition for flammable or explosive atmospheres containing gases, vapours, mists or combustible dusts. They are electrical equipment and static electricity.

Electrical equipment

Electrical equipment is covered by The Equipment and Protective Systems Intended for Use in Potentially Explosive Atmospheres Regulations 1996 (ATEX). They place duties on manufacturers/ suppliers to meet the Essential Health and Safety Requirements, to affix CE marking, and to state which equipment group (corresponding to the hazardous zones, shown below) the equipment or protective system belongs to.

There is a transitional period until 30 June 2003 before these Regulations come fully into force, but equipment bearing CE marking will be available before then. During this period, if CE-marked equipment is not available, you will need to select equipment to the relevant BS/BS EN standard or other equally effective standard.

Atmospheres containing flammable/explosive vapours

Where electrical equipment is installed and flammable or explosive atmospheres may be present, it is strongly recommended that these areas are classified into hazardous zones. British Standard 5345 provides guidance on this. Areas outside these zones are classified as non-hazardous. It is often less costly and safer to locate electrical equipment in these non-hazardous areas:

Zone 0: in which an explosive gas/air mixture is continuously present, or present for long periods;

Zone 1: in which an explosive gas/air mixture is likely to occur in normal operation;

Zone 2: in which an explosive gas/air mixture is not likely to occur in normal operation, and if it does, it will exist only for a short time.

30

Typical hazardous area classification where flammable liquids are used

Item	Extent of area	Classification
Store rooms and buildings.	Every part.	Zone 2
Open air storage.	Vertically to 1 m above top of highest container, and horizontally to 1 m beyond bund or sill.	Zone 2
Pump inside a building.	• Within any enclosure around the pump. • Within a horizontal radius of 4 m and vertically from ground level to 2 m above the unit.	Zone 1 Zone 2
Closed process vessel, filled and emptied by pipeline.	• Inside the vessel. • Vertically from ground level to 2 m above the vessel and horizontally to 2 m from the vessel (or to 1 m outside the sill if this is greater).	Zone 0 Zone 1
Open vessel.	• Inside the vessel. • Vertically from ground level to 1 m above the vessel and horizontally to 2 m from the vessel. • Horizontally to 2 m beyond the Zone 1 area (or to 1 m outside the sill if this is greater). Also vertically to a height of 3 m if the Zone 1 area does not reach 3 m in height.	Zone 0 Zone 1 Zone 2

To reduce the risk of the flammable/explosive atmosphere being ignited, any electrical equipment (including fixed and portable equipment) used in a hazardous zone should be constructed to a suitable explosion protected standard. Equipment with the appropriate CE marking or, during the ATEX transitional period, to BS 5345 or other equally effective standard, provide such protection. BS 5345 gives advice on selecting, installing and maintaining explosion protected electrical equipment.

Atmospheres containing combustible dusts

There is no current standard for the zoning of explosive atmospheres containing combustible dusts. Such dusts do not behave in the same way as gases. Maximum surface temperatures and dust ingress into electrical enclosures are more important. Surface deposits of dust may ignite on equipment that is designed to run hot, or may block ventilation holes or otherwise interfere with the cooling of electrical equipment. BS 6467 gives advice on the design,

selection, installation and maintenance of equipment for use in the presence of combustible dusts.

Try to site electrical equipment away from dusty areas. However if you need to install it in such a place, use a dust tight enclosure to prevent the risk of dust ignition inside the equipment. BS EN 60529 classifies enclosures for electrical equipment according to the protection they give against hazards such as ingress of water, dusts etc. (The dust tight standard is IP6X.)

To reduce the risk of ignition of explosible/ combustible dusts, the electrical equipment should either have the appropriate CE marking or, during the ATEX transitional period, be to the relevant BS/BS EN standard, or an equally effective standard.

31

Static electricity

The movement of liquids, eg during pumping, emptying, filling vessels, etc and the movements of other materials such as powders, can create a build-up of static electricity. When discharged, it can cause a spark that can ignite a flammable or combustible dust atmosphere.

To protect against static build-up check that the following points have been addressed:

❏ all metal and other conducting parts of equipment are adequately earthed before any liquids or powders begin to flow;

❏ all fixed equipment handling flammable liquids and combustible powders are electrically bonded together and earthed;

❏ earth continuity is checked regularly (at least annually);

❏ earthing contacts are maintained and kept clean;

❏ portable containers are earthed by wire to the fixed earthed plant;

❏ anti-static additives are used if necessary, where highly insulating liquids are processed.

RELEVANT LEGISLATION

Health and Safety at Work etc Act 1974

The Electricity at Work Regulations 1989

The Equipment and Protective Systems Intended for Use in Potentially Explosive Atmospheres Regulations 1996

RELEVANT GUIDANCE

Memorandum of Guidance on the Electricity at Work Regulations 1989 HS(R)25 HSE Books 1989 ISBN 0 11 883963 2

Maintaining portable and transportable electrical equipment HS(G)107 HSE Books 1994 ISBN 0 7176 0715 1

The safe use of portable electrical apparatus PM32 HSE Books 1990 ISBN 0 7176 0448 9

The safe use and handling of flammable liquids HS(G)140 HSE Books 1996 ISBN 0 7176 0967 7

Safe handling of combustible dusts: Precautions against explosions HS(G)103 HSE Books 1994 ISBN 0 7176 0725 9

Electricity at Work Regulations: Guidance for small businesses IND(G)89L HSE Books 1994

Safe working with flammable substances IND(G)227L HSE Books 1996 ISBN 0 7176 1154 X

-3-
CHEMICAL INDUSTRY ACTIVITIES

*This section covers some of the typical processes
and activities carried out by the chemical industry and gives guidance on
the action you may need to take. It covers:*

- *Storing hazardous substances*

- *Production*

- *Maintenance and modifications to plant and processes*

- *The finished product*

STORING HAZARDOUS SUBSTANCES

Virtually all chemical manufacturing and processing operations involve storing hazardous substances in the form of raw materials and finished products. Other operators solely or predominantly store chemicals. Proper storage of these substances is vital for the safe operation of your business. Inadequate storage has led to many serious incidents.

> *A fire and explosion destroyed a Salford warehouse and caused widespread damage to surrounding property. The warehouse stored a variety of chemicals including oxidising agents, flammable solids and flammable liquids. If the chemicals had been stored properly, the risk of the fire breaking out could have been greatly reduced.*

This part deals with two main types of storage:

● hazardous liquids in bulk tanks;

● hazardous substances in packages, eg drums, kegs, bags, etc.

First this part describes the steps that are common to the safe storage of hazardous substances in general. This is then followed by some of the more specific requirements of bulk and packaged storage.

Common issues

Step 1: Allocate the storage duties to an appropriate member of staff and ensure they are fully trained and competent in identifying, assessing, handling and storing the hazardous substances on site.

Step 2: Identify the properties of all hazardous substances to be stored, eg flammables, oxidising agents, corrosives, toxics, etc. Then obtain information on the storage requirements of those substances. This will include information on containment, neutralisation and cleaning up spillages, behaviour under fire conditions and any specific storage requirements such as separation or segregation needs. Useful sources of information are labels, safety data sheets, industry and HSE guidance.

Step 3: Decide on appropriate storage requirements and put them in place and ensure they are maintained. Make sure that any substances that may adversely effect each other in an incident, eg fire, leaks, etc aren't stored together. For example, if a fire breaks out in your store and oxidisers and flammables are stored together, the fire will be much more severe than if they were properly segregated. Further details on separating hazardous substances is given later on pages 38-39.

Step 4: Make sure that procedures are in place for dealing with any spillages. These should include:

❒ readily available information on the hazards of the substances stored;

❒ training staff in the correct way to deal with spillages, including the correct use of PPE;

❒ readily available PPE selected to fit the people who will clear up the spillages and of a high enough standard to give protection against the hazards of the substances stored;

❒ a supply of containers (eg bags, drums) and absorbent material for clearing up leaks and spills and a safe method of disposing of them.

Note: When deciding on such procedures you may find it useful to refer to pages 20-22.

Step 5: Prepare an emergency plan to deal with incidents such as fire and explosion. The plan will need to include the following:

❒ a list of substances in store (including quantities) and where they are in the store. This list will provide valuable information to the emergency services attending an incident and it will be useful to liaise with them so they know where to obtain the list;

❒ equipment for detecting and controlling a fire in the store such as heat/smoke detectors, sprinkler systems and fire extinguishers;

❒ training staff in the use of fire extinguishers;

❒ an evacuation procedure including notification to neighbours of any risks to them;

❒ making sure that the store is identified by appropriate safety signs;

❒ making sure that if you have more than 25 tonnes of a dangerous substance on site, you notify the fire authority, your health and safety authority and mark the site appropriately.

Note: When preparing the above plan, you may find it useful to refer to Section 4 on emergencies.

ACTIVITIES - STORING HAZARDOUS SUBSTANCES

Storing hazardous liquids in bulk tanks

The following points should be considered when storing hazardous liquids in bulk tanks.

☐ Are the materials the tank is made from suitable for the substance it is to contain? For example, mild steel is not suitable for dilute sulphuric acid and hydrochloric acid tanks must be rubber lined or made from stainless steel.

☐ Is the tank and its fittings protected from vehicle impact, eg from fork-lift trucks, delivery vehicles, etc? Crash barriers, kerbs, fixed bollards and well planned vehicle routes will help.

☐ Are there signs on the tank(s) and fill points to show its contents and hazardous characteristics? Accidents have happened when delivery drivers filled the wrong tank. Signs also help ensure your operators take the correct substances for the work being done.

☐ How do you prevent the tank from being overfilled? You should know the capacity of the tank and how much is in it before adding any more to it. Dipsticks, gauges, high level alarms or interlocked high level alarms should be used as appropriate. The higher the hazard of the liquid, the greater the level of overfill protection needed.

☐ Is access required onto the tank, eg for using dipsticks, or connecting filling pipes? Can gauges or low level filling points be used instead? If not, safe, secure access ladders and platforms need to be provided.

☐ When filling or drawing from the tank there may be a risk of exposure to the hazardous liquid, so what precautions do you take? PPE may be needed. Decide what items of PPE are needed, make sure they fit the user and are of a high enough standard to protect against the hazards of the liquid.

☐ Do you regularly inspect your storage tank(s) for signs of deterioration? This will help spot early signs of corrosion, leaking valves, taps, pipework, etc and will help reduce the risks to operators from handling contaminated equipment and clearing up leaks.

☐ Is the tank bunded to contain leaks and spillages? Bunding of tanks provides the following advantages:

- it contains the spilt liquid, minimises the release of vapour and so helps reduce exposure;

- it allows controlled recovery of spilled liquid;

- it prevents environmental contamination.

The volume of a bund should be 110% of the volume of the largest tank in the bund. Tanks containing incompatible substances should not be located in the same bund. A means of draining surface water from the bund will be required and the bund walls will need protecting from vehicle damage.

Tanks containing LPG and similar substances should not be bunded.

Additional points for storing flammable liquids in tanks

The main risk from flammable liquids is fire. The following points are aimed at reducing the risk of fire by keeping fuel and ignition sources apart (you may find it useful to refer to pages 10-14).

☐ It is preferable for tanks to be located outside so any flammable vapour given off is dispersed by the open air. Other locations may be used if specialist advice and extra precautions are followed.

☐ Tanks should be separated from ignition sources by the distances shown in the table on page 37:

Tank capacity		Minimum separation distance from any part of a tank	
Single tanks: m^3	Total for a group* (maximum): m^3	From building, boundary, source of ignition, filling point or process unit: m	From a bund wall m
Up to 1	3	1**	1
1-5	15	4	1
5-33	100	6	1
33-100	300	8	1
100-250	750	10	2
Above 250	-	15	2

*   A tank should be considered as part of a group if the distance from the tank to any other tank is less than the appropriate distance in column 3.

**   But at least 2 m from doors, plain-glazed windows, ventilation or other openings of means of escape. Also not below any opening (including building eaves and means of escape) from an upper floor, regardless of vertical distance.

☐   Try to site electrical equipment away from tanks storing flammable liquids. However, if electrical equipment has to be fitted near a flammable liquid storage tank, it will need to be constructed to a suitable explosion protected standard. Pages 29-32 on electricity gives advice on selecting such electrical equipment.

☐   Bunds are very important for containing flammable liquids. As well as the benefits already shown, they prevent the liquid from reaching ignition sources and stop the liquid spreading a fire around the site.

☐   LPG cylinders should be kept a minimum of 3 m from a flammable liquid tank or its bund and LPG vessels should be sited a minimum of 6 m from a flammable liquid tank or its bund.

Storing hazardous substances in packages

The following points should be considered when storing hazardous substances in packages, eg bags, drums, kegs, etc.

☐   Check that packages going into store have identifiable labels showing their contents and hazard? If they are unlabelled, don't put them into store until they are labelled.

☐   Do you check that all packages going into store are inspected for damage, leaks, etc? If not, you may be storing packages that could leak and contaminate other packages being stored.

☐   Where do you store the packages? They should preferably be stored in a dedicated storage building or an effectively fire separated compartment of a building.

The building needs to be made of non-combustible materials and be sited to minimise the risk to nearby premises both on and off site in the event of a fire.

☐   Do you know which substances can be stored together and which ones need separating or segregating?

It is essential that incompatible substances are kept apart so that:

●   if a fire occurs the rate of growth and intensity of the fire is minimised;

●   if a spillage occurs the chance of substances reacting together, causing more problems such as producing toxic substances, is minimised.

If specific advice on storing your substances is not available, the table on pages 38-39 gives a guide to separating and segregating substances. It is based on the labelling required on the substance for transport purposes.

KEY REFERENCE

The storage of flammable liquids in fixed tanks (up to 10 000 m^3 total capacity) HS(G)50 HSE Books 1990 ISBN 0 11 885532 8

SEGREGATION TABLE

The table shows general recommendations for the separation or segregation of different classes of dangerous substances.

CLASS		2 (Flammable Gas)	2 (Compressed Gas)	2 (Toxic Gas)	3 (Flammable Liquid)
COMPRESSED GASES 2.1 Flammable	2		KEEP APART	Segregate from	Segreg from
2.2 Non flammable /non toxic	2	KEEP APART		KEEP APART	KEE APAR
2.3 Toxic	2	Segregate from	KEEP APART		Segreg from
FLAMMABLE LIQUIDS	3	Segregate from	KEEP APART	Segregate from	
FLAMMABLE SOLIDS 4.1 Readily combustible	4	Segregate from	Separation may not be necessary	KEEP APART	KEE APAR
4.2 Spontaneously combustible	4	Segregate from	Segregate from	Segregate from	Segreg from
4.3 Dangerous when wet	4	Segregate from	Separation may not be necessary	KEEP APART	Segreg from
OXIDISING SUBSTANCES 5.1 Oxidising substances	5	Segregate from	Separation may not be necessary	Separation may not be necessary	Segreg from
5.2 Organic peroxides	5	ISOLATE	Segregate from	Segregate from	ISOLATE
TOXIC SUBSTANCES	6	KEEP APART	Separation may not be necessary	Separation may not be necessary	KEE APAR
CORROSIVE SUBSTANCES	8	KEEP APART	KEEP APART	KEEP APART	KEEP APAR

38

ACTIVITIES - STORING HAZARDOUS SUBSTANCES

4			5		6	8
FLAMMABLE SOLID 4	SPONTANEOUSLY COMBUSTIBLE 4	DANGEROUS WHEN WET 4	OXIDISING AGENT 5.1	ORGANIC PEROXIDE 5.2	TOXIC 6	CORROSIVE 8
Segregate from	Segregate from	Segregate from	Segregate from	ISOLATE	KEEP APART	KEEP APART
Separation may not be necessary	Segregate from	Separation may not be necessary	Separation may not be necessary	Segregate from	Separation may not be necessary	KEEP APART
KEEP APART	Segregate from	KEEP APART	Separation may not be necessary	Segregate from	Separation may not be necessary	KEEP APART
KEEP APART	Segregate from	Segregate from	Segregate from	ISOLATE	KEEP APART	KEEP APART
	KEEP APART	Segregate from	Segregate from	Segregate from	KEEP APART	Separation may not be necessary
KEEP APART		KEEP APART	Segregate from	ISOLATE	KEEP APART	KEEP APART
Segregate from	KEEP APART		KEEP APART	Segregate from	Separation may not be necessary	Separation may not be necessary
Segregate from	Segregate from	KEEP APART		Segregate from	KEEP APART	KEEP APART
Segregate from	ISOLATE	Segregate from	Segregate from		KEEP APART	KEEP APART
KEEP APART	KEEP APART	Separation may not be necessary	KEEP APART	KEEP APART		Separation may not be necessary
Separation may not be necessary	KEEP APART	Separation may not be necessary	KEEP APART	KEEP APART	Separation may not be necessary	

KEY

Separation may not be necessary — Separation may not be necessary, but suppliers should be consulted about requirements for individual substances. In particular, it should be noted that some types of chemicals within the same class may react violently, generate much heat if mixed or evolve toxic fumes.

KEEP APART — Separate packages by at least 3 m or one gangway width, whichever is the greater distance in the store room or storage compound outdoors. Materials in non-combustible packaging which are not dangerous substances and which present a low fire hazard may be stored in the 3 m space. At least this standard of separation should be provided between substances known to react together readily, if that reaction would increase the danger.

Segregate from — These combinations should not be kept in the same building compartment or outdoor storage compound. Compartment walls should be imperforate, of at least 30 minutes' fire-resisting construction and sufficiently durable to withstand normal wear and tear. Brick or concrete construction is recommended. An alternative is to provide separate outdoor compounds with an adequate space between them.

ISOLATE — This is used for organic peroxides, for which dedicated buildings are recommended. Alternatively, some peroxides may be stored outside in fire-resisting secure cabinets. In either case, adequate separation from other buildings and boundaries is required.

Where a particular material has the properties of more than one class, the classification giving the more onerous segregation requirements should be used.

ACTIVITIES - STORING HAZARDOUS SUBSTANCES

❑ How do you ensure the packages are safely stacked in the store? Is suitable racking available? Have you set standards for maximum stack size and height? Stack sizes may need to be limited to reduce the severity of a fire.

❑ Do you know the safe storage capacity of your store to make sure it doesn't become over-stocked?

❑ Safe stacking is essential to prevent packages falling and injuring people or damaging the packages causing spillages.

❑ How do you handle the packages in the store? Has manual handling been eliminated or reduced where possible? For example, depalletising standard 200 litre drums should not be done manually. Where fork-lift trucks are used, make sure the drivers are trained and the store is set out with enough room for them to be used safely. See page 23 for further information on manual handling.

❑ What steps have you taken to reduce the risk of a fire starting in the store? Using the information on pages 10-14 on fire will help decide what you need to do. Often the first material ignited in a fire is not a hazardous substance. For this reason it is strongly recommended that stocks of combustible materials (such as packaging) are not kept in stores with hazardous substances. You will also need to control ignition sources, eg smoking, maintenance work, heating systems, electrical supplies and equipment, etc.

Additional points for storing flammable liquids in drums

When storing flammable liquids in tanks, the main risk is fire. The following points are aimed at reducing the risk of fire by keeping fuel and ignition sources apart.

❑ Storage areas for drums containing flammable liquids are best outside because any flammable vapour given off can easily be dispersed. If it is not reasonably practicable to use an outside storage area, a suitable storeroom, preferably in a separate building, may be used. If such a storeroom is to be used, further advice and information on its construction and location needs to be obtained (see the second key reference on this page).

❑ An outside storage area needs to be secure to prevent trespassing or tampering and be separated from ignition sources by distances shown in this table.

Minimum separation distances	
Quantity stored: litres	Distance from occupied building, boundary, process unit, flammable liquid tank or fixed ignition source: m
Up to 1000	2.0
1000 - 100 000	4.0
100 000 - 300 000	7.5
Above 300 000	7.5

Notes:
1 The maximum stack size should be 300 000 litres, with at least 4 m between stacks.

2 Containers should not be stored within the bund of a fixed flammable liquid tank or within 1 m of a bund wall.

KEY REFERENCE
Storage of packaged dangerous substances
HS(G)71 HSE Books 1992 ISBN 0 11 885989 7

KEY REFERENCE
The storage of flammable liquids in containers
HS(G)51 HSE Books 1990 ISBN 0 7176 0481 0

❐ Try to site electrical equipment away from flammable liquid stores. However, if electrical equipment has to be fitted near such a store, it will need to be constructed to a suitable explosion protected standard. Pages 29-32 on electricity give advice on selecting such electrical equipment.

❐ Spillages from the storage area should be contained in a bund or a similar arrangement large enough to hold 110% of the contents of the largest drum.

❐ LPG cylinders need to be kept a minimum of 3 m from the drums (or bund) and LPG vessels need to be sited a minimum of 6 m from the drums (or bund).

Now using the information in this part, check your storage arrangements, identify any areas where you can make improvements, carry them out and check they have worked.

RELEVANT LEGISLATION

The Health and Safety at Work etc Act 1974

The Highly Flammable Liquids and Liquefied Petroleum Gases Regulations 1972

Dangerous Substances (Notification and Marking of Sites) Regulations 1990

RELEVANT GUIDANCE

The storage of flammable liquids in fixed tanks (up to 10 000 m³ total capacity) HS(G)50
HSE Books 1990 ISBN 0 11 885532 8

The storage of flammable liquids in fixed tanks (exceeding 10 000 m³ total capacity) HS(G)52
HSE Books 1991 ISBN 0 11 885538 7

Storage of packaged dangerous substances
HS(G)71 HSE Books 1992 ISBN 0 11 885989 7

The storage of flammable liquids in containers
HS(G)51 HSE Books 1990 ISBN 0 7176 0481 0

Storage and handling of industrial nitro-cellulose
HS(G)135 HSE Books 1995 ISBN 0 7176 0694 5

The safe use and handling of flammable liquids
HS(G)140 HSE Books 1996 ISBN 0 7176 0967 7

Safe working with flammable substances
IND(G)227L HSE Books 1996 ISBN 0 7176 1154 X

Dangerous substances (notification and marking of sites) guidance on regulations HS(R)29
HSE Books 1990 ISBN 0 11885435 6

Dangerous substances on site notification and warning IND(G)92(L) HSE Books 1990

Lift-trucks in potentially flammable atmospheres
HS(G)113 HSE Books 1996 ISBN 0 7176 0706 2

Keeping LPG in cylinders and similar containers
CS4 HSE Books 1986 ISBN 0 7176 0631 7

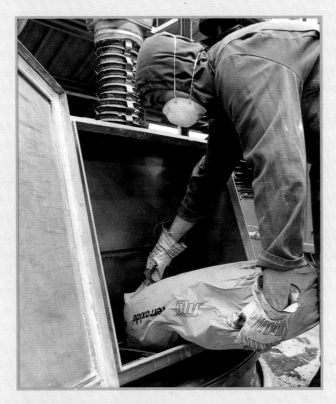

The information given in this part is not comprehensive but is typical of the areas you will need to consider when carrying out your own risk assessments.

One of the main problems in the chemical industry is the loss of containment of hazardous substances (ie, substances escaping). This can lead to fire, explosion and people being exposed to substances that may harm their health. Also fires and explosions can cause more loss of containment by damaging storage tanks, drums, reactors, etc.

Some sources of loss of containment and control measures are shown on the next page.

PRODUCTION

This part considers some typical operations carried out by chemical manufacturers and processors and shows some of the hazards, risks and control measures associated with them. It deals with them under the hazards of fire, explosion, work-related ill health and equipment and the workplace. The typical operations considered are:

- packing, eg bagging powders and granules, bottling and drumming liquids;

- mixing and blending materials;

- reactor operation;

- physical processing, eg drying, grinding and filtering operations.

SOURCE OF LOSS OF CONTAINMENT
(or how substances may escape)

- Inadequate equipment design for the work being carried out/processing being undertaken.

- Leaks from vessels, pumps, valves, bellows, pipework, etc, largely due to poor maintenance.

- Spillages, eg during bottling, bagging, drumming or when charging mixers, blenders and reactors, etc.

- Over-pressurisation of vessels such as reactors, and distillation columns, etc, resulting in the vessel contents venting through an over-pressure relief system or the vessel exploding.

- Maintenance work on equipment that has not been purged and cleaned of hazardous substances.

- Overfilling vessels and storage tanks.

- Operator error.

CONTROL MEASURES

- Accurate assessment of the equipment and the work to be carried out to ensure they are compatible.

- Preventative maintenance system.
- Trained and competent maintenance staff.

- Enclosed transfer systems.
- Workstations designed to minimise spillages.
- Trained and competent operators.

- Gauges, alarms controls, protection systems, for example to keep the vessel operating at the correct pressure, etc.
- Accurate operating instructions.
- Trained and competent operators.

- System to ensure equipment is purged and cleaned of hazardous substance before maintenance work starts. This will usually be in the form of a PTW system (see page 55).

- Gauges, alarms, accurate operating instructions.

- Trained competent operators.
- Clear accurate operating instructions.

ACTIVITIES - PRODUCTION

PACKING - Fire hazards

HOW RISKS MAY ARISE

- Ignition of a flammable atmosphere produced from vapours or dusts during packing operations, resulting in a fire.

- Ignition of a spillage of flammable liquid or solid, resulting in a fire.

- Fire in stocks of flammable material in the workroom.

CONTROL MEASURES

- Transfer of product being packed via an enclosed system with explosion relief panels eg pipelines, augers, etc.
- Use LEV, with explosion relief, panels to remove the flammable atmosphere.
- Eliminate/control ignition sources.

- Spillage retention sills and bunds.
- Planned safe spillage clear-up procedures.
- Eliminate/control ignition sources.

- Minimise stocks of flammable materials in the workroom to the amount needed for half a day or one shift's production.
- Keep the main stocks of flammable substances in a proper storage facility.
- Provide fire-fighting equipment suitable for materials in use and train employees in its use.

PACKING - Explosion hazards

HOW RISKS MAY ARISE

- Ignition of an explosive atmosphere produced from vapours or dusts during packing, resulting in an explosion.

- A secondary dust explosion caused by ignition of dust dislodged by the initial explosion, eg from ledges.

- Decomposition, resulting in an explosion, of energetic substances being packaged.

CONTROL MEASURES

- Transfer of product being packed via an enclosed system with explosion relief panels, eg pipelines, augers, etc.
- Use LEV, with explosion relief panels, to remove the explosive atmosphere.
- Eliminate/control ignition sources.

- Cleaning programme to prevent dust accumulating in the workplace.

- Ensure the material is not too sensitive to handle. Keep to safe operating conditions such as correct temperatures and avoid contamination of the substance.

44

PACKING - Work-related ill health hazards

HOW RISKS MAY ARISE

■ Exposure to hazardous substances such as irritants, toxics, corrosives which may occur by inhalation, ingestion, or skin absorption. A high risk area is when the substances are handled at the point of transfer from bulk supply into packages.

■ Injuries from manual handling of packages of bulk materials.

■ Injuries from manual handling of finished packages, eg packing boxes, stacking pallets. (Typically affecting the shoulders, arms and hands.)

CONTROL MEASURES

■ Transfer of products being packed via an enclosed system, eg pipelines, augers, etc.
■ LEV to reduce fumes and dust, etc.
■ Train staff in safe working procedures.
■ Personal protective equipment (PPE), eg gloves, face shield, respirators, etc, selected to fit the operators and protect them from the hazards of the substances handled.
■ Train users of PPE in its fitting, use and maintenance.

■ Mechanical transfer of bulk materials via pipelines, augers, etc.
■ Purchase materials in easily handled sized packages.
■ Use handling aids such as pallet trucks, hoists, drum handling equipment, etc.
■ Use team lifting techniques.

■ Design work stations to correct height reach distances and layout.
■ Use mechanical handling equipment, eg conveyors.
■ Train staff in safe lifting techniques.

PACKING - Equipment and workplace hazards

HOW RISKS MAY ARISE

■ Injuries from using machines, eg augers, conveyors, valves, pumps, etc, where dangerous parts such as auger inlets, drive belts, shafts, etc, are accessible.

■ Injuries from contact with moving vehicles, eg fork-lift trucks, delivery vans and lorries, etc.

■ Falling from storage hoppers and tanks, etc while checking levels or sampling the contents.

■ Injuries from slipping or tripping in the workplace.

CONTROL MEASURES

■ Guard dangerous parts to prevent access to them.
■ Train operators in the safe use of machines.

■ Separate pedestrian routes from vehicle routes.
■ Train the drivers. Avoid the need to reverse vehicles.

■ Use level gauges and low level sample points.
■ Provide fixed ladders, steps and platforms with hand and intermediate rails.

■ Good housekeeping and procedures for spillage clear-up.
■ Maintain equipment to prevent spillages.

MIXING AND BLENDING - Fire hazards

HOW RISKS MAY ARISE

- Ignition of a flammable atmosphere produced in and around the mixing/blending vessel, resulting in a fire.

- Ignition of a spillage of flammable liquid or solid, resulting in a fire.

- Fire in stocks of flammable material in the workroom.

CONTROL MEASURES

- Substitute flammable solvents, etc with less hazardous alternatives.
- Use sealed mixing/blending vessels, eg with close fitting lids to minimise the flammable atmosphere escaping from the vessel. The vessel may require venting.
- Use enclosed transfer systems, with explosion relief panels, to fill and empty the vessel.
- Use LEV, with explosion relief panels, to remove the flammable atmosphere.
- Inerting of the mixing/ blending vessel.
- Eliminate/control ignition sources.

- Spillage retention sills and bunds.
- Planned safe spillage clear-up procedures.
- Eliminate/control ignition sources.

- Minimise stocks of flammable materials in the workroom to the amount needed for half a day or one shift's production.
- Keep the main stocks of flammable materials in a proper storage facility.
- Provide fire-fighting equipment suitable for the materials in use and train employees in its use.

MIXING AND BLENDING - Explosion hazards

HOW RISKS MAY ARISE

- Ignition of an explosive atmosphere produced in and around the mixing/blending vessel, resulting in an explosion.

- A secondary dust explosion caused by ignition of dust dislodged by the initial explosion, eg from ledges.

- Decomposition, resulting in an explosion, of energetic substances being mixed/blended.

CONTROL MEASURES

- Substitute flammable solvents, etc with less hazardous alternatives.
- Substitute dusty materials with pastes, pellets, etc.
- Use a sealed mixing/blending vessel, eg with close fitting lid to keep explosive atmosphere and dusts in the vessel. The vessel may require venting.
- Inerting of the mixing/blending vessel.
- Use enclosed transfer system, with explosion relief panels, to fill and empty the vessel.
- Have extraction ventilation, with explosion relief panels, to remove explosive atmosphere and dusts.
- Eliminate/control ignition sources.
- Maintain all plant and pipework to minimise dust emissions.

- Cleaning programme to prevent dust accumulating in the workplace.

- Ensure the material is not too sensitive to handle. Keep to safe operating conditions such as correct temperatures, avoiding contamination of the substance and prevention of heating from the machinery, eg from bearings, mixing blades, etc.

46

MIXING AND BLENDING - Work related ill health hazards

HOW RISKS MAY ARISE

- Exposure to hazardous substances such as irritants, toxics, corrosives. This may happen by inhalation, ingestion or skin absorption, eg when filling or emptying the mixing/blending vessels, from fumes emitted from the vessel or when sampling the contents of the vessel.

- Injuries from manual handling when filling and emptying mixing/blending vessels.

- Noise levels produced by mixing/blending/milling equipment may be high enough to damage hearing.

CONTROL MEASURES

- Use enclosed transfer systems to fill and empty the vessel.
- Close fitting lids to keep fumes in.
- Use LEV to remove fumes and dusts, etc especially if the vessel is charged manually.
- Train staff in safe working procedures and good hygiene practice.
- Use appropriate PPE selected to fit the operator and protect them against the hazards of the substances handled.
- Train users of PPE in its use, fitting and maintenance.

- Mechanical transfer of materials to and from the vessel.
- Purchase materials in easily handled sized packages.
- Use handling aids, eg hoists, pallet trucks, drum handling equipment, etc.
- Train staff in safe lifting techniques.
- Use team lifting techniques.

- Fit noise reduction devices, eg sound deadened panels, materials, anti-vibration mountings, etc.
- Site equipment in a noise reducing enclosure.
- Site equipment away from workers.
- Use hearing protection selected for noise. levels produced and train workers in its use.
- Purchase quieter equipment in the future.

MIXING AND BLENDING - Equipment and workplace hazards

HOW RISKS MAY ARISE

- Access to dangerous parts of the mixing/blending vessels such as paddles, stirrers, etc when charging or sampling vessel content, can result in injuries.

- Gaining access to the mixing/blending vessel to charge it or sample from it may result in a trip or fall.

- Slipping on spilt materials.

CONTROL MEASURES

- Guard dangerous parts to prevent access to them. If access is required for sampling or adding materials, interlocked guards need to be used.

- Use a mechanical transfer system to remove the need for access.
- Provide fixed ladders, steps and work platforms with hand and guard rails.

- Maintain vessels to minimise leaks.
- Good housekeeping and procedures for spillage clear-up.

ACTIVITIES - PRODUCTION

REACTOR OPERATION

Many of the hazards, risks and control measures involved with the use of reactors are the same as for using mixing and blending vessels. Consequently the following list will deal with risks and controls required **in addition** to those on the list for mixing and blending operations.

REACTOR OPERATION - Fire hazard

HOW RISKS MAY ARISE

- Ignition of a flammable atmosphere in and around the reactor. The flammable atmosphere may come from raw materials, intermediate and finished products of the reaction.

CONTROL MEASURES

- Inerting of the reactor.
- Accurate process operating instructions identifying when a flammable atmosphere is likely to be present.
- Eliminate/control ignition sources, in particular from the source of heat for the reactor.

REACTOR OPERATION - Explosion hazard

HOW RISKS MAY ARISE

- Explosion of the reactor due to inadequate equipment and process design for the process being carried out.

CONTROL MEASURES

- Accurate assessment of the equipment and the process to ensure they are compatible, eg does the design allow for adequate heat transfer from the reaction? Is there sufficient cooling and back-up coolant, etc?
- Substitute hazardous materials with safer ones.
- Use semi-batch operation where materials are added over time instead of all at once.

- Explosion of the reactor due to a rise in pressure beyond the reactor's capability. For example, during a runaway exothermic reaction or decomposition of an unstable chemical.

- Accurate process operating instructions designed to keep reaction under control.
- Train operators.
- Use appropriate instruments, control and protection systems to monitor and control the reaction to keep it within specified limits or safely shut it down.
- Use appropriate protection systems such as: crash cooling; reaction inhibition; quenching; secondary containment; pressure relief devices (eg pressure relief valves, bursting discs), etc.

- Explosion due to failure of the reactor vessel.

- Regular examination of the reactor vessel and pressure relief devices by a competent person.
- Regular maintenance of the reactor vessel and protection systems.

48

REACTOR OPERATION - Work-related ill health hazards

HOW RISKS MAY ARISE

■ Exposure to hazardous intermediate and final products of the reaction, eg when adding materials, sampling the contents or emptying and cleaning the reactor.

CONTROL MEASURES

■ Accurate process instructions identifying the hazards and precautions required when adding materials, sampling or cleaning, etc.

■ Use enclosed transfer systems for adding materials.

■ Use appropriate PPE selected to fit the operator and protect against the hazards of the substances to which they are exposed.

REACTOR OPERATION - Equipment and workplace hazards

HOW RISKS MAY ARISE

■ Burn injuries from contacting hot or cold parts of the reactor.

CONTROL MEASURES

■ Lag exposed hot or cold parts.

PHYSICAL PROCESSING - Fire hazards

HOW RISKS MAY ARISE

- Drier heating contents above its ignition temperature, resulting in a fire.

- Ignition of a flammable atmosphere given off when filtering flammable liquids, resulting in a fire.

CONTROL MEASURES

- Accurate operating instructions for the dryer.
- Temperature controls and gauges on the dryer.
- Appropriate control and protection systems to keep the temperature below its ignition temperature or safely shut the dryer down. (In order to set safe operation temperatures, you will need adequate information on the material being processed.)

- LEV to remove flammable atmosphere.
- Eliminate/control ignition sources.
- Provide fire-fighting equipment suitable for the materials in use and train employees in its use.

PHYSICAL PROCESSING - Explosion hazards

HOW RISKS MAY ARISE

- Grinding of solids into powders, granules, etc, can create a combustible dust cloud which, if ignited, may explode.

- A secondary dust explosion caused by ignition of dust dislodged by the initial explosion, eg from ledges.

- Decomposition, resulting in an explosion, of energetic substances being processed.

CONTROL MEASURES

- Prevent overheating caused by flow blockages or poor maintenance of equipment.
- Prevent foreign matter entering the mill.
- Eliminate/control ignition sources.

- Design new plant and buildings to avoid surfaces where dust may accumulate, where practicable.
- Cleaning programme to prevent dust accumulating in the workplace.
- Seal equipment to reduce dust emissions.
- Use LEV to reduce dust emissions.

- Ensure the material is not too sensitive to handle, keep to safe operating conditions such as correct temperatures, avoiding contamination of the substance and prevention of over-heating from the machinery, eg from bearings, mixing blades, etc.

PHYSICAL PROCESSING - Work-related ill health hazards

HOW RISKS MAY ARISE	CONTROL MEASURES
Handling substances into and out of filters, dryers, grinders, etc, can expose operators to irritant, corrosive, toxic substances, by inhalation, ingestion or skin contact.	Train staff in safe working procedures. Use LEV to reduce dust and fumes. Use enclosed transfer systems, eg pipelines and augers. Use appropriate PPE selected to fit the user and protect them from the hazards of the substances handled.
Exposure to hazardous substances when removing filter cake from filters.	Use appropriate PPE selected to fit the user and protect them from the hazards of the filter cake.
Exposure to dust from grinding operations.	Seal grinder to reduce dust emissions. Use LEV to reduce dust. Use an appropriate respirator/dust mask.
Injuries from manual handling when loading and emptying dryers, grinders, filters, etc.	Mechanised transfer systems. Manual handling aids, eg hoists, pallet trucks, etc. Use team lifting techniques Manual handling training.
Noise levels from grinding machines can be high enough to damage hearing.	Enclose grinder in noise reducing enclosure. Site grinder away from workers. Use hearing protection selected for noise levels produced. Purchase quieter equipment in the future.

PHYSICAL PROCESSING - Equipment and workplace hazards

HOW RISKS MAY ARISE	CONTROL MEASURES
Injuries from accessing dangerous parts of machines, eg grinders.	Guard dangerous parts. If lids of grinders form part of the guarding, they need to be interlocked.
Burns from hot parts of machines, eg dryers.	Lag exposed parts.
Falling when gaining access to fill and empty dryers, grinders, filters, etc.	Use mechanical transfer systems to remove need for access. Provide fixed ladders, steps, work platforms with hand and guard rails.

Remember, these lists do not cover all risks and control measures of the operations listed but are typical of the areas to consider when carrying out your own risk assessments.

For relevant legislation and guidance please refer to the appropriate sections of this booklet.

MAINTENANCE AND MODIFICATIONS TO PLANT AND PROCESSES

Many incidents in the chemical industry come from operations not directly involved in production. Examples are maintenance of plant (including cleaning, repairing and servicing), and modifications to plant and processes which may include new items of plant.

This part of the book looks at maintenance and modifications to plant and processes.

Maintenance

Plant needs to be maintained to keep it in a safe working condition. This means maintenance is carried out to prevent problems arising (preventive maintenance) and to put faults right after a breakdown (breakdown maintenance).

Before any maintenance work is carried out, it needs to be properly planned and the risks assessed so that it can be done safely and without compromising the safety of the plant.

> *Two fitters suffered serious burns when sprayed with 98% sulphuric acid while removing an accumulator from an acid pump. Pressure on the discharge side of the pump had not been vented, though the permit indicated the line had been cleared.*

Preventive maintenance

Preventive maintenance allows you to close down the plant at a convenient time and clean it out before starting on the maintenance work, making it safer for those doing the work. This also allows the work to be done at the most convenient time in the production cycle and should reduce the amount of breakdowns and lost production you suffer.

Breakdown maintenance

Carrying out breakdown maintenance when the plant fails can lead to problems such as breaking into contaminated plant and making temporary repairs to keep the process going. This involves more risk for those doing the work and often leads to lost production.

Carrying out as much planned preventive maintenance as you can is a safer and usually a more cost-effective option.

When carrying out maintenance some of the main points to consider are shown on page 53.

KEY REFERENCE
Dangerous maintenance: A study of maintenance accidents and how to prevent them
HSE Books 1992 ISBN 0 11 886347 9

ACTIVITIES - MAINTENANCE AND MODIFICATIONS

Who will do the maintenance work - your staff or contractors?

❑ If contractors are used they may not be familiar with your site or processes and will need to be informed of any hazards on site that may affect their work and any company procedures or rules they must follow, eg emergency procedures, permits-to-work, or procedures for bringing equipment on to site.

❑ You will need to establish how the contractor is going to carry out the work (eg by a method statement) and whether it will introduce new hazards on to the site which may put your staff at risk.

Is there a risk of fire?

❑ If the work involves plant that contains or has contained flammable substances, these substances should be removed or reduced to a minimum, and any supply of flammable substances to the plant needs to be isolated.

❑ Sources of ignition need to be controlled, eg by using non-sparking tools, permits-to-work (PTWs), a no smoking policy, etc.

Is there a risk of explosion?

❑ If the work includes being in or near a potentially explosive atmosphere, this atmosphere needs to be removed or reduced to below the lower explosive limit and the source of the explosive atmosphere isolated.

❑ Any energetic substances (ie those that can decompose, resulting in fires or explosions) that could be affected by the work being done need to be removed.

❑ Sources of ignition need to be controlled, eg by using non-sparking tools, PTWs, a no smoking policy, etc.

❑ If the work is on a pressurised vessel or pipeline it needs to be depressurised and the source of pressure (eg compressed air, gases and steam) isolated.

Is there a risk of ill health?

❑ If the work could involve exposure to a hazardous substance (eg cleaning out tanks, mixers, and repairing contaminated plant), the substance needs to be removed and the plant washed through. Where substances aren't totally removed, appropriate PPE may be needed. The source of the substance to the plant also needs to be isolated.

❑ If the work involves manually handling heavy items of plant, appropriate lifting aids need to be used.

Is there a risk from machinery or gaining access to the plant?

❑ If plant being worked on has moving parts (eg mixing paddles, grinders) isolate the power source to them.

❑ If the plant being worked on is not safely accessible from existing work platforms, appropriate safe temporary access will be needed, eg scaffold, mobile hydraulic work platforms, etc.

Could the work involve entry into a confined space?

❑ Entry into confined spaces such as tanks and reaction vessels is a high risk activity and should be avoided. For example, it may well be possible to do the job from outside or remotely. You will need to consider these options when assessing the risks from the work and planning how it is to be done. However, if from your assessment of the risks, entry into the confined space cannot be avoided, you will need to make special provisions for a safe system of work, drawing up strict precautions, and rescue plans in the event of an emergency. Further information is given on page 54.

KEY REFERENCE
Managing contractors: A guide for employers
HSE Books 1997 ISBN 0 7176 1196 5

KEY REFERENCE
Hot work, welding and cutting on plant containing flammable materials HS(G)5
HSE Books 1979 ISBN 0 11 883229 8

ACTIVITIES - MAINTENANCE AND MODIFICATIONS

Confined spaces

The precautions needed are best laid down in writing in the form of a PTW. Details of these are given later.

The safe system of work will need to cover the following:

❏ the level of supervision. It may well be necessary to appoint a responsible person to supervise the work. They would need to operate the PTW system, check that the precautions are being followed and ensure that proper instructions are given;

❏ isolating the vessel to stop dust, fume or hazardous substances getting in. Mechanical and electrical equipment within the confined space may also need to be isolated. Further information on isolation is given later;

❏ cleaning/removing residues to ensure fumes do not develop while the work is being done;

❏ testing the atmosphere. Check that it is free from toxic or flammable vapours. Usually you need further monitoring to check that there is enough fresh air available as the work is carried out;

❏ if flammable or toxic gases are present, purging with air or inert gas may be necessary, then test the atmosphere before entry. Mechanical ventilation of the confined space may also be necessary to replace air used up during work and to remove fumes produced;

❏ selecting equipment. If there is a risk of a flammable atmosphere, electrical equipment needs to be of an explosion protected standard. The electrical section gives details - see pages 30-31. Also, static electricity is a source of ignition and some equipment may need earthing. Non-sparking tools may also be needed. Even if there isn't a flammable atmosphere, you may also need to select appropriate lighting, (eg low voltage lighting protected against knocks and suitable for damp conditions) and PPE (eg breathing apparatus);

❏ not using petrol/diesel equipment inside the confined space;

❏ safe access into and out of the confined space. Are the size of the openings adequate?

Emergency procedures need to cover:

❏ the rescue equipment needed. For example, it is very unlikely that someone on their own would be able to lift or rescue a person using only a rope;

❏ an adequate communication system. Whatever system is used, eg speech, tugs on a rope, telephone, radio, etc, it is important that all messages can be understood quickly and clearly. This includes contact with people outside the confined space who need to raise the alarm and start rescue procedures;

❏ training of the rescuers in the likely causes of emergencies and how to use the equipment provided, such as breathing apparatus, safety lines, etc. Multiple fatalities have occurred when rescuers have been overcome by the same conditions that affected the person being rescued;

❏ involvement of the emergency services. They will want all the information you have about the confined space before they carry out a rescue.

PTWs and isolation of plant form essential parts of a safe system of work for many maintenance activities - the key points of them are shown on pages 55-56.

New regulations on entry into confined spaces are likely to come into force in 1997.

KEY REFERENCE
Entry into confined spaces GS5
HSE Books 1995 ISBN 0 7176 0787 9

Permits-to-work (PTW)

☐ PTW systems are used to control types of work which are identified as potentially hazardous. For maintenance work this includes situations where work can only be carried out if normal safeguards are removed or new hazards introduced, eg entry into confined spaces, hot work, pipeline breaking.

☐ The PTW system should have written instructions showing how it works and what jobs it is used for.

☐ A PTW form is used to help control the work. This should specify clearly the actual work to be done, the hazards of the work and precautions to be taken, eg isolation and PPE.

☐ The issuer of the PTW form should fully understand the hazards and precautions associated with the proposed work and be trained in using the PTW system. Users of PTW forms should also be trained on how the system works.

☐ The PTW system should include a procedure for checking the work and handing the plant back to production staff once the maintenance work is completed.

☐ The design of the PTW form should take into account the specific conditions and require-ments of your workplace and processes. You may require different forms for different tasks, eg hot work, entry into confined spaces, etc.

The diagram below shows the essential requirements of a PTW form.

1 **Permit title.**

3 **Job location.**

4 **Plant identification.**

6 **Hazard identification** - including residual hazards and hazards introduced by the work.

7 **Precautions necessary** - person(s) who carries out precautions, eg isolations, should sign that precautions have been taken.

8 **Protective equipment.**

9 **Authorisation** - signature confirming that isolations have been made and precautions taken, except where these can only be taken during the work. Date and time duration of permit.

11 **Extension/shift handover procedures** - signatures confirming checks made that plant remains safe to be worked upon, and new acceptor/workers made fully aware of hazards/precautions. New time expiry given.

2 **Permit number.** Reference to other relevant permits or isolation certificates.

5 **Description of work to be done and its limitations.**

10 **Acceptance** - signature confirming understanding of work to be done, hazards involved and precautions required. Also confirming permit information has been explained to all workers involved.

12 **Hand back** - signed by acceptor certifying work completed. Signed by issuer certifying work completed and plant ready for testing and recommissioning.

13 **Cancellation** - certifying work tested and plant satisfactorily re-commissioned.

KEY REFERENCE
Chemical manufacturing: *Permit-to-work systems* IND(G)98(L) HSE Books 1992

55

ACTIVITIES - MAINTENANCE AND MODIFICATIONS

Isolating equipment

❏ Hydraulic or pneumatic powered equipment, eg valves, etc should be first isolated at the valves and then the supply and return pipes disconnected. Any stored energy in the system should be released beforehand. If necessary, provide bleed valves and pressure gauges to help check that the pressure has been released.

❏ Isolate engine powered equipment by shutting off the engine fuel supply and then dis-connecting and isolating all starting systems.

❏ Isolate electrically powered equipment by using switch disconnectors, removing plugs from socket outlets or removing fuses, all secured by using locking off devices.

❏ Where equipment has been isolated but may still move, eg by gravity, use a chock or scotch to lock it in a safe position.

Isolating chemical and pressurised plant

The greater the hazard of the plant and process, the more certain the method of isolation needed. The methods of isolation available in descending order of safety are:

● physical disconnection and blanking, where a length of pipe or fitting is removed so there is a physical gap in the pipeline. The end of the pipework connected to the source is then blanked off;

● spades or line blinds, where a solid plate (ie spade, slip plate etc) is physically inserted and secured in position at a flanged joint of a pipeline effectively blocking it;

● double block and bleed, where a bleed valve is fitted between two valves and isolation is achieved by closing the two valves and draining the connecting section of pipe via the bleed valve. The drawback of this method is that there may be leaks past the main valves and bleed valves can become blocked, resulting in poor isolation;

● closed and locked valves. Remember, valves may leak and this method is usually only suitable for work where there is little or no risk and involving low hazard fluids.

Modifications to plant and processes

If you need to modify your plant or processes, the modifications need to be designed by competent personnel and a risk assessment carried out on the proposed modifications. This assessment will identify the effects they will have on health and safety and will enable a safe design to be made. Formal procedures such as HAZOP's (Hazard Operability Studies) are available for this process and can help you identify significant hazards and make improvements at the design stage.

> *The residues tank of an aniline recovery still corroded away, leaking over half a tonne of residues. The plant was originally made of stainless steel, but the residues tank was a modification and had incorrectly been made of mild steel, which corroded.*

The main points to consider are the following:

❏ if a process is changed or a new process introduced on existing plant, the chemistry of the process will need to be checked to make sure it will work safely;

❏ trials may need to be completed in the laboratory and/or on a pilot plant after the chemistry has been checked;

❏ does the modification take the existing plant beyond what it was designed to do, and if so, can the plant still operate safely?

❏ does the modification affect any control devices, eg valves, gauges, agitation speed and cooling water flow?

❏ does the modification affect any safety devices, eg relief valves, alarms, sensors, vent size?

❏ will operating instructions and training of operators need updating?

☐ has the modification affected access to the plant, eg for valve operation, means of escape, etc?

☐ has bringing back the plant into use been planned? You need to check the modification has been installed as designed and operates safely before bringing the plant to full production;

☐ do not forget to amend the plant and process records following any modifications.

So take a planned approach to maintenance and modifications, reduce the risk of injuries and minimise disruption to production.

RELEVANT LEGISLATION

The Health and Safety at Work etc Act 1974

The Management of Health and Safety at Work Regulations 1992

The Provision and Use of Work Equipment Regulations 1992

The Factories Act 1961, Section 30

RELEVANT GUIDANCE

Dangerous maintenance: A study of maintenance accidents and how to prevent them HSE Books 1992 ISBN 0 11 886347 9

Cleaning and gas freeing of tanks containing flammable residues CS5 HSE Books 1985 ISBN 0 11 883518 1

Entry into confined spaces GS5 HSE Books 1995 ISBN 0 7176 0787 9

Hot work, welding and cutting on plant containing flammable materials HS(G)5 HSE Books 1979 ISBN 0 11 883229 8

Guidance on permit-to-work in the oil industry (Oil Industry Advisory Committee Guidance Book) HSE Books 1991 ISBN 0 11 885688 X

Work equipment: Guidance on regulations L22 HSE Books 1992 ISBN 0 7176 0414 4

Managing contractors: A guide for employers HSE Books 1997 ISBN 0 7176 1196 5

Chemical manufacturing: *Permit-to-work systems* IND(G)98L HSE Books 1992

THE FINISHED PRODUCT

This part explains what you need to do once you have produced the finished products and are ready to supply them to your customers. There are three areas to consider:

❏ safe storage (covered in pages 34-41);

❏ supplying information and packaging the goods for the safety of the users of your products;

❏ supplying information and packaging the goods for safety while the goods are being transported.

Information and packaging for users

If you supply hazardous chemicals you need to provide sufficient information to enable users of the chemicals to identify the hazards of the chemicals and take appropriate steps to protect their health and safety. If the chemicals are supplied in packages (as opposed to bulk, eg via tanker or pipeline), they need to be packaged so they can be handled safely.

An operator was badly burnt in an explosion after a cobalt alloy powder was charged into a reactor containing water. No labels or information were provided to warn about the hazard of adding the powder to water.

The following shows the main steps you need to take.

Step 1: Decide if your chemicals are hazardous, eg are they toxic, corrosive, etc. A full list of danger categories is given in the table on page 59. In most cases, if your chemicals aren't in one of these categories they aren't considered dangerous.

Step 2: If your chemicals are hazardous you have to classify them into the appropriate category of danger to help provide the correct information and packaging. There are three ways to decide the classification of your chemicals:

❏ use the classification given to the chemical by your supplier, provided it is accurate and still valid for the chemical after you have processed it;

❏ use the classification given in the *Approved supply list* (3rd edition). This list is produced by HSE and covers most common chemicals but not mixtures of chemicals;

❏ if you can't classify by the above two ways, you will have to classify them yourself by collecting relevant information. Detailed guidance on this classification procedure is given in HSE's publication *The approved guide to the classification and labelling of substances and preparations dangerous for supply* (2nd edition).

KEY REFERENCE
CHIP 2 for everyone HS(G)126
HSE Books 1995 ISBN 0 7176 0857 3

58

CATEGORIES OF DANGER

	Category of danger	Indication of danger	Symbol
Physico-chemical	Explosive	Explosive	
	Oxidising	Oxidising	
	Extremely flammable	Extremely flammable	
	Highly flammable	Highly flammable	
	Flammable	Flammable	
Health	Very toxic	Very toxic	
	Toxic	Toxic	
	Harmful	Harmful	
	Corrosive	Corrosive	
	Irritant	Irritant	
	Sensitising	Harmful	
		Irritant	
	Carcinogenic *Categories 1 and 2*	Toxic	
	Category 3	Harmful	
	Mutagenic *Categories 1 and 2*	Toxic	
	Category 3	Harmful	
	Toxic for reproduction *Categories 1 and 2*	Toxic	
	Category 3	Harmful	
Environmental	Dangerous for the environment	Dangerous for the environment	

ACTIVITIES - THE FINISHED PRODUCT

Step 3: Once you have classified your chemicals you can move on to providing information on them. This information has to be in two forms, a safety data sheet and a label.

Note: Label requirements only apply to chemicals supplied in packages.

☐ You have to provide a safety data sheet for any hazardous chemical you supply (whether in bulk or packages) if it is to be used in connection with work. The information has to be provided under the following 16 headings and needs to be sufficient to allow the user to decide on the precautions required when using the chemical.

☐ If you supply the hazardous chemical in a package, it must be labelled to inform anyone handling the package or using the chemical about the hazards and give brief advice on suitable precautions to take. The main information that has to be on the label is:

- supplier's name, address and phone number;
- the name of the chemical;
- indication of danger and the associated symbol (see the table on page 59);
- appropriate risk phrases;
- appropriate safety phrases.

1	Identification of the substance/preparation and company.	9	Physical and chemical properties.
2	Composition/information on ingredients.	10	Stability and reactivity.
3	Hazards identification.	11	Toxicological information.
4	First-aid measures.	12	Ecological information.
5	Fire-fighting measures.	13	Disposal consideration.
6	Accidental release measures.	14	Transport information.
7	Handling and storage.	15	Regulatory information.
8	Exposure controls/personal protection.	16	Other information.

The label needs to be easy to read and securely fixed to the package - examples of two labels are shown here.

NITRIC ACID

Oxidising

Corrosive

Contact with combustible material may cause fire
Causes severe burns
Keep locked up and out of reach of children
Do not breathe vapour
In case of contact with eyes rinse immediately with plenty of water and seek medical advice
Wear suitable protective clothing
In case of accident or if you feel unwell, seek medical advice immediately (show the label where possible)

EEC Label 231-714-2

Supplied by:
Burge, Brown and Richardson Ltd
Mahony Mansions, Old Feret Road,
London, United Kingdom
Tel: 0000-1111-2222

Example of a supply label for a substance. This product would have child-resistant closures and tactile danger warnings fitted if offered for sale to the public.

UNCLE MURRAY'S PATENT CLEANSER
Contains trichloroethylene

Harmful
1 litre

Possible risk of irreversible side effects
Do not breathe vapour
Keep out of reach of children
Wear suitable protective clothing and gloves

Supplied by:
Burge, Brown and Richardson Formulations Ltd
Mahony Tower, Royal Allen Road, Ford Industrial Estates
London, United Kingdom
Tel: 0000-1111-2222

Example of a supply label for a preparation. This product would have a tactile danger warning fitted if offered for sale to the public.

KEY REFERENCE
Safety data sheets for substances and preparations dangerous for supply (2nd edition)
HSE Books 1994 ISBN 0 7176 0859 X

60

Step 4: If you supply the hazardous chemical in packages, you need to ensure that:

- ☐ the packaging is designed, constructed, maintained and closed to prevent any of the contents escaping when subjected to stresses and strains of normal handling;

- ☐ the packaging is not made of materials that could be adversely affected by the chemical;

- ☐ any chemicals you supply to the public labelled very toxic, toxic or corrosive that have reclosable packaging are fitted with a child resistant closure;

- ☐ any chemicals you supply to the public labelled very toxic, toxic, corrosive, harmful, extremely flammable, or highly flammable have a tactile danger warning (usually a small raised triangle) attached, to alert the blind and partially sighted.

When these steps have been carried out, you can despatch the chemicals following the guidance below on transport.

Information and packaging for transport

This part only deals with transport by road. If you transport by rail, air or sea, further advice will probably be needed.

Transporting goods by road involves the everyday risks of traffic accidents. The transportation of dangerous goods, eg those classified as toxic, flammable, etc, adds further hazards such as fire, chemical burns and explosions.

> *The rear wheel of a lorry carrying drums of a toxic corrosive liquid caught fire, the fire extinguisher couldn't cope and the fire spread to the load. Nine people including four fire-fighters were taken to hospital. No written information (which could have alerted the fire brigade to use breathing apparatus) about the load was being carried.*

This part looks at what you need to do to reduce the risks when transporting dangerous goods.

Action is required by all those involved in the transport operation, from the consignor of the goods (usually the manufacturer), and the operator of the transport business to the driver of the vehicle itself.

As a manufacturer, you will almost certainly be involved in consigning goods and may well run your own transport.

The main aims are to transport the goods in packages and vehicles designed to minimise leakage in the event of an accident and to provide information about the hazards of the load for the emergency services.

The main steps you need to take are:

Step 1: Consignors of dangerous goods have to classify them according to their most hazardous properties in relation to transporting them. Many goods are already classified in the *Approved carriage list*. For those not in this list you will have to collect the relevant information and classify them yourself. Detailed guidance on this is given in HSE's publication *Approved requirements and test methods for classification and packaging of dangerous goods for carriage.*

The classification may differ from the one given for the benefit of users because the transport hazard may be different. For example, with a corrosive substance that is also toxic over a long period of exposure, its toxicity may be more relevant to users and its corrosive nature more relevant to those transporting it.

The classification then helps in the labelling and packing of the goods.

Step 2: Consignors of dangerous goods in packages need to ensure that:

- ☐ the packages are of good quality and constructed to prevent any leakage that may result from normal transport conditions, eg handling, stacking, dropping;

- ☐ the packaging is made of materials that won't be adversely affected by its contents.

In many cases this will mean the use of type approved packaging designed and tested to UN or similar standards. Further information on type approved packaging is available from the Department of Transport.

KEY REFERENCE
Are you involved in the carriage of dangerous goods by road or rail?
IND(G)234L HSE Books 1996
ISBN 0 7176 1258 9

61

Step 3: Consignors of dangerous goods in packages have to label them to inform those dealing with an incident (eg a leak or road accident) involving dangerous goods, what the hazards are and what goods they are dealing with. In most cases, the label needs to show:

- the name of the goods;
- the UN number of the goods;
- the appropriate danger sign;
- any subsidiary hazard sign.

A typical label is shown below - note the danger sign is a diamond shape for easy recognition. Labels for user information are square. Combined labels showing transport and user information can be used and will show both warning signs.

Step 4: Consignors of dangerous goods, whether in bulk or packages, have to provide written information to the operator of the transport. The information to be provided is the:

- identity of the goods;
- quantity to be carried;
- nature of the hazards created by the goods and the action to be taken in an emergency.

Step 5: Operators must ensure the vehicles used for the transport, eg road tankers, container lorries, etc are suitable for the goods being carried and where appropriate, are equipped with suitable fire-fighting equipment. This usually consists of two fire extinguishers, one in the cab and the other on the lorry.

Step 6: Operators must ensure that, where appropriate, vehicles carrying dangerous goods are marked with the relevant hazard warning panels.

Step 7: Operators must ensure the drivers of vehicles transporting dangerous goods have received adequate training on the hazards created by the goods carried and the action to take in an emergency. Part of the training will usually involve the driver passing a test and obtaining a Vocational Training Certificate (VTC) relevant to the dangerous goods being carried.

Step 8: Operators must pass the written information from the consignor to the driver.

Step 9: Drivers of vehicles carrying dangerous goods need to:

❏ keep the written information about the load readily available at all times and make sure any written information about other dangerous goods is removed from the vehicle or kept in a securely closed container to prevent confusion in an incident;

❏ follow the training given about the load, including fire precautions and carry their VTC with them;

❏ make sure the hazard warning panels are displayed when appropriate and kept clean and clear of obstructions.

If these steps are taken, your goods should be transported safely and if there is an incident, information will be available to help the emergency services.

Note: In respect of packaged goods some of the above steps only apply when the quantities carried exceed the limits set out in the Carriage of Dangerous Goods by Road Regulations 1996. These limits vary according to the level of risk associated with the goods carried.

RELEVANT LEGISLATION

The Health and Safety at Work Act 1974

The Chemicals (Hazard Information and Packaging for supply) Regulations 1994 (CHIP 2)

The Carriage of Dangerous Goods by Road Regulations 1996 (SI 2095)

The Carriage of Dangerous Goods (Classification, Packaging and Labelling) and Use of Transportable Pressure Receptacles Regulations 1996 (SI 2092)

The Carriage of Dangerous Goods by Road (Driver Training) Regulations 1996 (SI 2094)

The Carriage of Explosives by Road Regulations 1996 (SI 2093)

The Carriage of Dangerous Goods by Rail Regulations 1996 (SI 2089)

The Packaging, Labelling and Carriage of Radioactive Material by Rail Regulations 1996 (SI 1996 Number 2090)

The Health and Safety at Work etc. Act 1974 (Application to Environmentally Hazardous Substances) Regulations 1996 (SI 1996 Number 2075)

RELEVANT GUIDANCE

CHIP 2 for everyone HS(G)126 HSE Books 1995 ISBN 0 7176 0857 3

Approved guide to the classification and labelling of substances and preparations dangerous for supply (2nd edition) HSE Books 1994 ISBN 0 7176 0860 3

Safety data sheets for substances and preparations dangerous for supply (2nd edition) L62 HSE Books 1994 ISBN 0 7176 0859 X

Approved supply list (3rd edition) CHIP '96 (database included) L76 HSE Books 1996 ISBN 0 7176 1116 7

The complete idiot's guide to CHIP 2 IND(G)181L HSE Books 1995

Why do I need a safety data sheet ? IND(G)182L HSE Books 1994

Read the label: How to find out if chemicals are dangerous IND(G)186L HSE Books 1995

Approved carriage list L90 HSE Books 1996 ISBN 0 7176 1223 6

Approved methods for the classification and packaging of dangerous goods for carriage by road and rail Carriage of Dangerous Goods by Road and Rail (classification, packaging and labelling) Regulations 1994 L53 HSE Books 1994 ISBN 0 7176 0744 5

The approved requirements and test methods for the classification and packaging of dangerous goods for carriage L88 HSE Books 1996 ISBN 0 7176 1221 X

The approved vehicle requirements L89 HSE Books 1996 ISBN 0 7176 1222 8

The approved tank requirements L93 HSE Books 1996 ISBN 0 7176 1226 0

The approved requirements for the packaging, labelling and carriage of radioactive material by rail L94 HSE Books 1996 ISBN 0 7176 1227 9

The approved requirements for the construction of vehicles for the carriage of explosives by road L92 HSE Books 1996 ISBN 0 7176 1225 2

The approved code of practice on the suitability of vehicles and containers and limits on quantities for the carriage of explosives L91 HSE Books 1996 ISBN 0 7176 1224 4

Guidance for consignors of dangerous goods by road and rail (classification, packaging, labelling and provision of information) HS(G)160 HSE Books 1996 ISBN 0 7176 1255 4

Guidance for road vehicle operators and others involved in the carriage of dangerous goods by road HS(G)161 HSE Books 1996 ISBN 0 7176 1253 8

Guidance for rail operators and others involved in the carriage of dangerous goods by rail HS(G)163 HSE Books 1996 ISBN 0 7176 1256 2

Guidance for operators, drivers and others involved in the carriage of explosives by road HS(G)162 HSE Books 1996 ISBN 0 7176 1251 1

Guidance for consignors, rail operators and others involved in the carriage of radioactive material by rail HS(G)164 HSE Books 1996 ISBN 0 7176 1257 0

-4-
EMERGENCIES

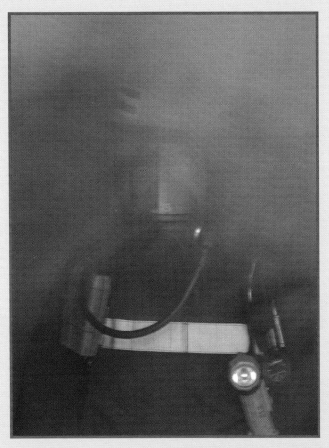

Even after assessing the risks from your business and taking appropriate precautions to control them, you should be prepared for an emergency situation and plan how you would deal with it. The aim is to contain and control an incident to minimise the effect of it on your employees and others who may be affected by it.

EMERGENCIES

The following points will help you decide what you should do to prepare for an emergency.

☐   Consider what incidents may occur and the circumstances in which they may arise, eg:

- fire;
- explosion;
- uncontrolled releases of gases or vapours;
- runaway exothermic reactions;
- spillages/leaks of chemicals.

Consider the consequences and the risks to people both on and off site, then decide what is required to minimise the effect of any incident.

Consider what improvements you can make to reduce the risks and what facilities, such as fire extinguishers, are required to help contain an incident.

When you have decided what precautions are needed, you should prepare written procedures, which may be quite simple, to deal with the emergencies you have identified.

☐   Your procedures need to cover:

- when and how the alarm is to be raised;
- how early assessment of the incident will be carried out, to decide on the action needed;
- who will be in charge until the emergency services arrive and where the emergency will be co-ordinated from. You will need access to a telephone;
- who does what at each stage of the emergency;
- the immediate action required to contain the incident;
- liaison with the emergency services and other off-site authorities, such as the local casualty department, who may need to be involved;
- providing information to the emergency services as soon as they arrive at the incident, eg information on the dangerous substances involved in the incident;
- how out of hours emergencies are to be dealt with;
- preventing access of non-essential people to the area;
- notifying nearby sites which may be affected by the incident;

KEY REFERENCE
Chemical manufacturing: *Prepared for EMERGENCY!* IND(G)155L HSE Books 1993

66

- evacuation or sheltering of non-essential workers depending on the type of incident, eg fire or toxic gas cloud;
- accounting for site workers, visitors and contractors;
- shutting down process equipment and making it safe;
- isolating the source of leaks or spillages and clearing them up in a safe manner;
- access to records, eg safety data sheets, stocklists/inventories and records of who is on site;
- in the event of an accident information to accompany the injured person to hospital, eg safety data sheet.

☐ Make sure everyone on site knows what to do if they:

- hear or see an alarm;
- discover a fire, leak or spillage;
- discover an injured person;
- experience a major plant or services failure.

☐ Your staff will need to be trained on the content of your emergency plans and practice them to ensure they work. Remember to include:

- relief and standby operators;
- maintenance staff and contractors;
- those working nights or weekend shifts;
- new employees;
- refresher training for all staff especially if the site changes, eg new plant is installed, new processes carried out, new buildings are used.

☐ Practices should be realistic exercises in the workplace and include any PPE that would be needed in an emergency, eg breathing apparatus, chemical suits, etc.

☐ Check that:

- there are enough emergency exits for everyone to get out easily;
- escape routes are clearly marked and unobstructed;
- alarms are tested regularly and can be heard over normal background noise;
- enough fire extinguishers of the right type are available to deal with small fires promptly. Your local fire authority will advise on the fire extinguishers you should have;
- those expected to use fire extinguishers are adequately trained.

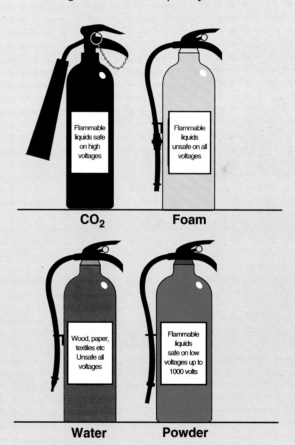

Flammable liquids safe on high voltages

Flammable liquids unsafe on all voltages

CO$_2$ **Foam**

Wood, paper, textiles etc Unsafe all voltages

Flammable liquids safe on low voltages up to 1000 volts

Water   **Powder**

☐ Discuss your emergency procedures with the emergency services so they can advise on any particular needs you may have and are aware of what you do on site.

☐ If you have more than 25 tonnes of a dangerous substance on site you must notify the fire authority, your health and safety enforcing authority and mark the site appropriately.

EMERGENCIES

First aid

You will need:

☐ a first aider or an appointed person available whenever people are at work. A first aider is someone who has passed an HSE approved first aid course. An appointed person is someone you authorise to take charge of an incident, eg to contact the emergency services. The number of first aiders required will depend on how many people you employ and the hazards and risks in your workplace, but remember you will need cover for shift work, sick leave and holidays;

☐ adequate facilities and equipment to give first aid to people injured or ill at work. The facilities and equipment should be appropriate for the hazards and risks in your workplace;

☐ to inform your employees where the first aid facilities and equipment are located and who the appointed people or first aiders are.

The key reference at the bottom of this column gives guidance on the equipment, numbers of appointed people or first aiders you require.

Reporting injuries and other events

All employers and the self-employed have to report certain injuries and incidents to their health and safety enforcing authority.

The main points are that you must:

☐ notify HSE immediately, normally by telephone, if anybody dies, receives a major injury or is seriously affected by, eg an electric shock or poisoning, and within 10 days follow this up with a completed accident report form (F2508);

☐ notify HSE immediately if there is a dangerous occurrence, eg a fire or explosion which stops work for more than 24 hours, or an overturned crane, and within 10 days follow this up with a completed accident report form (F2508);

☐ report within ten days (on form F2508) injuries which keep an employee off work or if they are unable to do their normal job for more than three days;

☐ report certain diseases suffered by workers who do specified types of work as soon as possible on learning about the illness. Use form F2508A;

☐ if you supply, fill or import flammable gas in reusable containers notify HSE immediately of any death or injury connected in any way with the gas supplied and confirm the notification with a report on F2508 within 14 days.

☐ keep a record of the incident, eg in an accident book.

KEY REFERENCE
First aid at work Health and Safety (First Aid) Regulations 1981 Approved Code of Practice COP42 HSE Books 1990 ISBN 0 7176 0426 8

KEY REFERENCE
Everyone's guide to RIDDOR'95 HSE 31 HSE Books 1996 ISBN 0 7176 1077 2

RELEVANT LEGISLATION

The Health and Safety at Work etc Act 1974

The Management of Health and Safety at Work Regulations 1992

The Health and Safety (First Aid) Regulations 1981

The Reporting of Injuries, Diseases and Dangerous Occurrences Regulations 1995

The Dangerous Substances (Notification and Marking of Sites) Regulations 1990

The Health and Safety (Safety Signs and Signals) Regulations 1996

RELEVANT GUIDANCE

Chemical manufacturing: *Prepared for EMERGENCY!* IND(G)155L HSE Books 1993

First aid at work Health and Safety (First Aid) Regulations 1981 Approved Code of Practice COP42 HSE Books 1990 ISBN 0 7176 0426 8

First aid at work: General guidance for inclusion in first aid boxes IND(G)4 HSE Books 1987 ISBN 0 7176 0440 3

First aid needs in your workplace: Your questions answered IND(G)3L(rev) HSE Books 1990

Emergency actions for burns IND(G)161L HSE Books 1994

Guide to Reporting of Injuries, Diseases and Dangerous Occurrences Regulations 1995 L73 HSE Books 1996 ISBN 0 7176 1012 8

Everyone's guide to RIDDOR '95 HSE 31 HSE Books 1996 ISBN 0 7176 1077 2

Notification and marking of sites The Dangerous Substances (Notification and Marking of Sites) Regulations 1990 HS(R)29 HSE Books 1990 ISBN 0 11 885435 6

Dangerous substances on site: Notification and warning signs IND(G)92L HSE Books 1990

Management of health and safety at work: Management of Health and Safety at Work Regulations 1992 Approved Code of Practice L21 HSE Books 1992 ISBN 0 7176 0412 8

Safety signs and signals: Guidance on regulations L64 HSE Books 1996 ISBN 0 7176 0870 0

QUESTIONNAIRE

FORMULA *for* HEALTH & SAFETY
GUIDANCE FOR SMALL AND MEDIUM-SIZED FIRMS IN THE CHEMICAL INDUSTRY

To help us assess this publication, will you please complete and return this questionnaire to the address overleaf. Postage is free.

We may wish to contact a sample of respondents with a fuller survey in future. If you do not wish to be contacted again please tick this box ☐

Mr, Mrs, Ms, Dr, Other _____ Initials _____ Surname _____

Position _____

Name of business _____

Address _____

_____

Postcode _____ Telephone _____ Fax _____

Size of business?   (Number of employees)
Fewer than 5 ☐   5 - 10 ☐   10 - 20 ☐   20 - 50 ☐   50 - 100 ☐   100 - 250 ☐   Over 250 ☐   Self-employed ☐

What is your main business? Manufacturing:

Paints, varnishes or inks	☐	*Soaps, toiletries & household preparations*	☐
Pharmaceuticals	☐	*Industrial & agricultural chemicals*	☐
Specialised fine chemicals	☐	*Other (please specify)*	☐

How did you hear about this publication?

Advertisement	☐	*HSE Inspector*	☐	*Trade Association*	☐
HSC Newsletter/News Bulletin	☐	*HSE Catalogue*	☐	*Mailshot*	☐
Local authority	☐	*Informal business contact*	☐	*Other (please specify)*	☐

Did you find the publication:

clear and straightforward?			*difficult to understand?*
1	2	3	4

Was the publication:

too technical?			*not technical enough?*
1	2	3	4

Was the publication:

well presented?			*poorly presented?*
1	2	3	4

Do you feel that the publication represents:

very good value?			*poor value for money?*
1	2	3	4

Was the publication helpful to you in identifying the health and safety risks associated with the work you do:

very useful			*not useful?*
1	2	3	4

Was the advice in the publication useful to you in identifying ways of controlling health and safety risks associated with your work:

very useful			*not useful?*
1	2	3	4

Did the publication help you to understand your responsibilities for health and safety:

very well	*well*	*a little*	*not at all?*
1	2	3	4

How much of the advice was relevant to the work you do:

all	*most*	*some*	*none?*
1	2	3	4

Any other comments _____

Thank you for taking the time to answer these questions

EC

FIRST FOLD

B

SECOND FOLD

BUSINESS REPLY SERVICE
Licence No. LV 5189

2

Health and Safety Executive
Room 303, Daniel House
Stanley Precinct
BOOTLE
Merseyside L20 3QY

EC

THIRD FOLD

A

Tuck A into B to form envelope
Please do not staple or glue

Printed and published by the Health and Safety Executive   C80   1/97